Heaven
&
Earth

How it all Works

Tonya Gamman

Heaven and Earth: How it all Works
Copyright © 2010 Tonya Gamman

Published by **New Swan Books**
Issaquah, WA 98027
www.newswanbooks.com

For further information, please contact tonyaswan@msn.com

Book cover design by Nancy Lee

ISBN 13: 978-0-9667511-1-6

Printed in the United States of America

Dedication

This book is dedicated to every one of you beautiful souls because we are all evolving and awakening to who we really are together. My hope is that this book will be another step forward in that process for many. It is also dedicated to my spiritual teachers, the masters of Earth's schoolroom, who have gone before us and left footprints for us to follow and a light to show us the way home when we finish our time here on our wonderful planet.

Acknowledgment

I would like to first acknowledge my teacher Kuthumi because much of what is in this book he taught me; my husband, Paul for all of his loving support and hours of editing and reviewing, not to mention sharing his wife with a book for eight years; my birth children: Reva, Maria, Jeremiah, Joshua, Clare, Michael-Sean, Alex, and my children from another mother: Brittany, Dustin, Alex, Austin, and Conner, for their encouragement and lovingly giving up time with me while I finished the work; my mother, JoAn for always being there, no matter what; my friend, Elizabeth Prophet and Saint Germain, who insisted I write it in the first place; Nancy Lee for the beautiful book cover artwork; and, last but not least, my editors: Wayne Purdin, Marcia McCarry, Ruth Matelich and Toddie Downs. I could not have done this without all of you. And all my dear friends and clients who encouraged me to keep going and finish it, I am so grateful to you and to all the others who contributed to the making of this book, both those in heaven and those on Earth.

Foreword
by
Wayne H. Purdin

As one of the editors of this book, I am in a position to write this foreword with some breadth of understanding, since I have read the manuscript several times. I am also a friend of the author.

This book helped my family and me even before it was published. As I began the final edit, my wife's mother died suddenly of a heart attack less than six months after her husband of 58 years died. I read parts of the final draft to my wife and daughters, in which Tonya describes what happens after death and what heaven is like. It comforted us and gave us a broader perspective on our loss.

Heaven and Earth: How it all Works is not just someone's recollection of heaven in a near-death experience (NDE) or out-of-body (OOB) trip. It's a past-life, death, between-life, life, and OOB account that weaves profound teachings about heaven and Earth into a personal story of two lifetimes that goes far beyond the brief glimpses and teachings gained in NDEs.

The story begins with a detailed account of the tragic last days of Tonya's previous life in 19th-century Ireland. Tonya traveled to Ireland to visit the very castle she lived in during that short life. Thus this chapter is rich in details that are usually not found in a past life memory. She then condenses 141 years in heaven into one chapter that describes heaven in exquisite detail and explains the major activities that souls engage in: healing, resting and reflecting, reviewing their last life, planning their next life, and preparing for reembodiment. One revelation that shatters the caricature of heaven is that there are no angels with wings sitting around strumming harps. What some people feel or see as angels are usually the souls of friends and relatives who come down occasionally to help. Tonya herself was mistaken for an angel when she came down to heal someone. Another misconception about heaven that Tonya clears up is that no one is judged for his or her wrong words, thoughts, and deeds, but everyone is given a life review in which they experience the pain they may have caused others. As Tonya writes in the Introduction, "In truth, we are the ones who do the 'judging.' We decide what we want to continue and what we want to change, based on love for ourselves, the true souls that we really are, and those we hold dear."

Tonya describes how a returning soul visits old haunts on Earth before entering a baby's body. When she enters her body, she says, "I'm like a pilot checking out my plane before takeoff, I activate systems and organs that are not working at full capacity. I am at the control center where I review all systems, body development, and functions." Soon after being born, Tonya forgets about heaven and the plans she has for this life. But when she is baptized at 11, she reconnects to the feeling of unconditional love, peace, and freedom that is heaven and to a "presence" who she calls "God."

Six months later, after practicing a meditation involving focusing on the point between waking and sleeping, she enters a state of heightened awareness and sees the presence as a being of light with brown eyes that are soft, deep and full of compassion. She writes, "His presence seems to pierce through to my soul, causing me to feel deeply loved and honored... He is emanating love, kindness, and an energy that is so strong, I feel as if I were being electrified with love, a love that penetrates every cell of my being... I somehow know that I have found my spiritual teacher; he is the presence that has been with me since the baptism. I feel we have been together forever and ever for an eternity of lifetimes. I am excited to meet him at last. His name is Kuthumi or the master K.H."

Kuthumi takes Tonya in her soul body to etheric retreats and cities of light in the heaven world for a series of lessons about life that lasts over a year. Tonya condenses the most important lessons she can remember into two chapters. Some of the lessons are personal as when she views scenes from her past lives in her "life book" (actually more like a holographic computer screen) in a vast library called "the hall of records." Other lessons are for the reader's edification as well, such as: everything is energy, the iceberg analogy for understanding difficult people, the merit system, we're all creators, and we all know the truth.

When Tonya's mother finds out about her daily excursions to cities of light with Kuthumi, she demands that she stop, even after taking her to a psychiatrist, who declares that she's just a normal, imaginative 12-year-old. Tonya reluctantly agrees and discontinues her OOB travels with Kuthumi. Over the next seven teenage years, she successfully navigates past pitfalls such as smoking, drugs, and alcohol, and accelerates her education (enrolling in college at 16) thanks to the lessons she learned from Kuthumi.

At 19, after a health crisis that ends her first marriage and her college education, she begins reading the lives of saints and discovers that others had similar experiences of masters and the heaven world. In one book, she is shocked and delighted to find a picture of Kuthumi, but the caption reads "Saint Francis of Assisi." None of the books about Saint Francis explain his role as a master teacher or his relationship to her. The end of the book is the beginning of her search for answers, a search that will take her through 33 more years of her life in a future sequel.

Contents

THE BATTLE · MY BROTHER AND I · A VISIT FROM MR. MOORE · TRAGEDY STRIKES · WISH I WERE DREAMING · MEETING EDWARD · OUTLANDISH IDEAS · THE GREAT ESCAPE · DREAM FROM THE PAST · EDWARD'S ENGLAND · FROM WEDDING TO WAR · NO GOODBYE FOREVER · REALIZATION DAWNS · TRUTH REVEALED · A WAY OUT

HEAVEN, HOME AT LAST · HEALING TEMPLE · MY LIFE REVIEW· THE PLACE OF REEMBODIMENT · DEVACHAN · SOUL GROUP MEETING · MY FAMILY GROUP · PLANNING MY NEXT LIFE · PREPARING FOR EMBODIMENT· MY MISSION GROUP · MY HEALING WORK IN HEAVEN · COMMUNICATION · ANIMALS · ANGELS · RETURN TO EARTH · PREPARING THE BABY BODY

MY SISTER MARY'S REBIRTH · GETTING A NEW BODY · MARY'S RETURN · MY GRANDFATHERS FUNERAL · THE BAPTISM · MEETING "THEM" · MY FAMILY · TERESA AND THE AURAS

"All the world's a stage, and all the men and women merely players: they have their exits and their entrances; and one man in his time plays many parts, his acts being seven ages." - William Shakespeare, *As you like it*

Prologue

From beginning to end, one's life seems to be a true mystery, full of grand learning experiences and intriguing questions.

- Do we really get only one life or is life a continuum?

- What am I doing here?

- Why did I come to this intense planet?

- Do I have a mission or a plan?

- Do the things I experience here happen as coincidental events?

- Is my life planned out in infinite detail before I even arrive?

- Is there a God?

- Do angels and guides exist or am I in this game of life alone?

These are some of the questions many people have asked themselves regarding their lives. Usually the answers are kept a secret from us while we live on this wondrous planet. This is the story of one who remembers the answers.

Introduction

When I was 11 years old, I had the great opportunity to meet a master teacher and learn from him directly about Heaven and Earth, how it all works. The knowledge I received has been of great value to me throughout my life. However, it was not my intention to share this information with others.

Then in1993, my life almost ended in a heart attack. At that time, a presence and light enfolded me. It told me my time on Earth was over, but that I was being given a life extension of four years. When the four years were drawing to a close, I wanted to stay here with my husband and seven children so I prayed fervently to be given more time. In a miraculous way, I was granted that extension with the stipulation that I write this book and thereby share my teacher's message with others.

His message is this: what it is really like in the heaven world and why we are here on Earth. This message is important because it relieves the guilt perpetuated by many erroneous human ideas especially those concerning judgment and karma.

My teacher's inspiration and insights, given to me throughout my life, are more than I have written in this book. I chose the ones I felt would be most valuable and wrote them in story form based on my own life experiences. His teachings gave me a broader perspective from which I could understand my life and navigate the challenges. My hope is that it will do the same for you.

Please note that there is a short glossary in the back of the book to assist you in understanding my terminology. I suggest reading it first. Also, the first chapter is based on my past life memory. In order to make it easier for you to follow, I have given names to the characters and places in that story.

It was and is my greatest pleasure to converse with one of Heaven's master teachers because he loves me like no embodied person, completely and totally unconditionally. Please savor this wonderful glimpse into the Heaven world and the liberation of his messages.

Thank you for joining me on this path of discovering who we really are. Enjoy your journey and I look forward to meeting you in Heaven or on Earth, if not in our dreams in between.

Abundant Blessings,

Tonya Gamman

The Battle of Waterloo by Robinson

CHAPTER ONE - MY PAST LIFE IN IRELAND

THE BATTLE

I am standing on the hillside watching as a battle rages before me. I am appalled and shocked at what I see unfolding before my eyes. It is the most horrible thing I have ever seen; men are screaming as they are stabbed to death or shot at close range. Their cries of anguish echo across the battlefield and strike my ears like a slap in the face. The pungent smoke of burnt gunpowder fills my nostrils and burns my eyes. The stench of death in the air makes my stomach turn.

"Where is the glory in this?" I think to myself. "And why am I here?"

Suddenly my attention is drawn to a small group of men fighting desperately for their lives. In the midst of them, one man catches my attention. He stands tall and brave. When I see him my heart falls. "O my God, it's him, the love of my life!" I begin to pray with all my heart that somehow no harm will come to him. "God, hear my prayer, please spare my beloved! Please bring him home to me!"

I pray as I have never prayed before in my life. As I plead with God to bring my love back home to me, the enemy closes in around him and his men. They are completely surrounded. I realize then that he will not escape and watch in anguish as my beloved is slaughtered. After a blow to his head, he lies still on the cold ground, and my life seems to drain out upon the earth with his.

I awake in a cold sweat, relieved that this was only a nightmare. As I open my eyes and think about my plans for the day, the horrible images of my dream fade away. By the time I am dressed, all that's left is a vague disquiet that casts a shadow over the joyful anticipation of my afternoon jaunt with my brother James.

"James," I whisper, "saddle the horses! I'll meet you at the stables." I sneak into the kitchen pantry to grab some bread and cheese for our afternoon snack. James is waiting with both horses already saddled as I reach the stables on the far side of the castle.

He has his favorite rogue stallion, and I my sweet-natured Irish mare. I wish I could ride his horses, but it is not allowed. "You are a lady, Katherine," my mother would say, "and ladies should ride safe, gentle horses." Often I walk by our extensive and beautiful stables and admire the powerful expensive horses owned by my family. I resent being limited to riding the safe horses.

James and I walk the horses to the falcon house where he retrieves his favorite bird, Jasmine. She is a sleek, silvery beauty. I can hardly contain my excitement at being able to go on an outing with my brother. It seems like he has been gone so long on "political business," as he calls it. Although he is five years my senior, we have always been close. For me, the sun rises and sets on my brother, and he shares my feelings. There is an understanding between us not shared by any of the other members of our household. We both have inquisitive minds and love to talk about questions that no one knows answers to, such as where man comes from, who God is, and other deep and intriguing topics. Many of our conversations are about spiritual ideas.

We also share a love of horses, falcons, music, and nature. That is another reason for our friendship. He married recently and now has a family to attend to, as well as his political work. This makes his visit today even more special. He acknowledges me with a knowing smile, holding our prize falcon on his arm. We mount and ride gently past the grove of trees into the open field. Here we are out of sight, far away from our house and the watchful gaze of our parents.

When we finally stop, I say, "I am famished. Would you like some bread and cheese?" So we rest for a few minutes and eat as we talk about our lives since we last saw each other. When we finish, he begins to work with the bird. Fortunately, we are out of sight and can do as we please. So far, no one has caught him allowing me to fly the family falcons. James began letting me work with the birds early in my childhood because I loved them so much. The birds respond well to me. I can handle any of them. Even the most difficult birds become calmer in my presence because they feel safe.

James takes off the falcon's hood and she rockets upward, then dives above our heads. It is thrilling to see the speed at which she can dive. What an incredible sight! We watch as our falcon swoops and dives, repeating her intricate and powerful sky dance. For several moments, James and I stand spellbound watching when a large white falcon comes into view. It flies with our bird circling above us. The feeling I get watching this bird gives me chills that reverberate through my body like waves on a pond. I just know that it is a spirit bird. According to legend, they foretell important events to come. I wonder what is heralded by the presence of this incredible beauty. A wonderful blessing, I assume. What a fortunate omen for our day together. Then our falcon whisks by us like a streak of silver, circles around, and lands on my outstretched arm.

I am so grateful not only to see James but also to get out of the castle and back into nature. I always feel the happiest here, but am never allowed to go by myself. As we mount our horses and start back for the castle, I plead, "Please, you must come and see me again soon. You know mother and father will not allow me to go without you." They do not consider it safe for me to go alone, so I only get to go when James is visiting. I look forward to these outings with great expectation. Lately, they have happened much less frequently than when he lived at home. Now that he has his beautiful wife and two children, he can't take the time off for riding and falconry on a regular basis, as he was wont to do when we were growing up.

"You know I will if I can, Katherine, but my life is not my own anymore. But I promise you, I will be back just as soon as I can." He smiles his best brotherly smile, as his eyes sparkle with delight at the idea. In that moment, my love for him is boundless. My heart feels light as we ride along, talking to each other.

Although my family owns Kilkenny castle and all the land around it, I sometimes feel like a prisoner in my own home. The grounds surrounding the castle are incredibly beautiful and well cared for. Kilkenny itself is considered to be one the most beautiful towns in all of Ireland. It is May and the grounds are full of colorful flowers and foliage. The surrounding countryside looks as if it had been painted with a lush green paintbrush. It is truly a paradise.

Kilkenny Castle

I am thankful for every minute I get to spend with James. He is an important man with important things to do. However, all I can think of is how it was when we were younger and how much fun we used to have. Why does he have to grow up and assume such heavy responsibilities? Why does he have to live somewhere else with his wife, Elizabeth? I love her very much, but I resent her taking my brother away.

Elizabeth is one of the most beautiful women in all of Ireland, and is admired by many men. She, however, loves only my brother. I love her for that and because she shares another passion I also share with my brother – music. She plays the piano like an angel, my brother is quite adept at the violin, and I am a fabulous harpist. It's something I practice quite regularly, since as a girl, I have little else to do. We often play together at family gatherings and for our own entertainment. One other reason I love her is that she has the cutest darling babies, my little niece and nephew, whom I adore.

We return to the stables and dismount. The servants take the horses and we walk back toward our house. Tonight my brother will be staying over for longer than usual because a dear friend of his is in town.

A VISIT FROM MR. MOORE

His name is Thomas Moore, and he also shares our love of music. He particularly loves to listen to me play the harp. Inspirational, he calls it, which pleases me greatly. Often, he makes up lyrics for our tunes and sings them as we play. His entire visit is so much fun that time flies by quickly. All too soon, he will have to leave for London or abroad. Then we will not see him again for months or years. I always feel so sad when he leaves. Often, when he is in Kilkenny, he takes a walk by the River Nore, where I can see him from inside our house. I watch him from our window whenever I can and wish that I could go out and talk with him. His mind is so deep and his ideas so interesting that I never tire of listening to him talk. He is much older than I, closer to my brother's age, a large thick man, exceptionally jolly, and always so very nice to me.

Today, we are preparing for a dinner with Mr. Moore and some military people from London. They are our houseguests tonight. I love to have guests and listen to their stories of what is going on in the world. My sister-in-law is attending and we are going to play some music for them after dinner.

Walking through the halls, I look up at the pictures of my relatives on the wall and wonder what they were like and how they liked living in this big castle. Most of them have long since passed on, before I was born, but I have heard stories about them all my life, so I feel like I know them. At 16, I still have so many questions about life. I thought when I grew up, that I would know all the answers. But actually life now seems even more confusing and I have more questions than ever.

When I reach the dining room, the guests stand until I am seated at our huge table. It is hard to see them because the table is so long and they are seated on the same side as I am. There is an older man who seems to be about 40, a younger soldier, perhaps 25 years old and two young soldiers who appear to be 18 or so. The 25-year-old stares at me as I come in and sit down. He seems nice enough, but I don't get to talk to him because he is too far away for comfortable conversation.

Dinner is served and we all enjoy ourselves. Afterwards, we retire to the living room and play music. The soldier who I am introduced to is Edward. He still seems entranced by my presence. Every time I look at him, he seems to be looking at me. I try to pretend I don't notice. I don't think much of it because harp music is so captivating. He probably loves my music, as have many other guests. After the entertainment, everyone retires. James and his wife take their carriage home. They don't live far from us, and I am grateful for that. I am happy to retire to my room and read.

TRAGEDY STRIKES

Later that evening, I hear people shouting and running around. There is a tension in the air that tells me something is very wrong. I dress quickly and come into the hall just in time to see my father rush by. He seems more upset than I have ever seen him before.

When I finally get downstairs, the men of our house, the military guests, and most of the servants are riding away on horseback. I stand there bewildered, wondering what is happening and where everyone is going. From the bits of conversation I hear, I am able to ascertain that something has happened at my brother's house, and that is where the riders are headed. The very thought of it fills me with a cold terror.

Much later, my father and the others return. First, my father talks to my mother privately in the drawing room downstairs. I can hear her sobbing from my room. Listening to the tone of their conversation and the intensity of her sobs, I know something terrible has happened. My sister, Mary, who has the room next to me, comes into my room for comfort. She is older than I am, but always seems to depend on me for answers.

"What do you think happened?" she asks.

"I don't know, but whatever it is, it's very bad," I reply apprehensively.

The next moment, we hear a door slam and my mother crying hysterically in her room. We listen with our ears to the door as my father talks to the servants and men waiting in the parlor. What he explains, we wish we had never heard. He says that my brother's house was broken into by a band of uprisers who killed James, his wife, and their two children in their beds. My father and the others captured the murderers and they have been imprisoned.

This news sends me into a state of shock. I can't believe what I hear; it can't be true. My brother, who I love so dearly, is gone and will never grace me with his beautiful smile and companionship again. I scream from the pain I feel in my heart and begin to weep. It seems as though the world is falling apart and will soon end for good. Life without my brother is no life at all. He is all that is good in my life, all I look forward to, my

11

only true joy. My sister and I hold each other and sob for hours until sleep finally overtakes us from exhaustion.

WISHING I WERE DREAMING

When I awake in the late morning, I feel as though I have been having a nightmare. Then the memory of the night before comes clearly into focus in my mind. My brother is dead. What should I do, I wonder? What cruel fate is this that took him from me without warning? Just yesterday we rode together, flew our falcon, and enjoyed an evening with guests playing music. He was alive and well. I can't accept that he is dead, gone forever from my life.

At breakfast, which is served much later than normal, the whole story comes out as I listen to the military men talking about what had happened the night before. My mother does not come to breakfast as she usually would. I don't feel much like eating either, but it seems better than sitting in my room. The details of the event make little difference to me. All that matters is that my brother is gone.

MEETING EDWARD

This time, the guests are seated in such a way that I can get a good look at them. Edward watches me constantly, although he does try not to stare. After breakfast, I go to stand at the window overlooking the river. Edward approaches me and offers his condolences about my brother's death. We speak for a while about the happenings of the night before. He fills in the details for me. A servant had come from my brother's house, explaining that there was trouble there; strange men had broken in. He had gone for help quickly before they saw him. My father rushed to my brother's house, followed closely by the soldiers and servants, only to find my brother and his family already dead. They pursued the uprisers, finally overtaking and capturing them.

He says my father wanted to kill all of them right then and there, but he was constrained by the wishes of the others. Killing them would not have returned my brother and his family to us. The uprisers were turned over to the authorities. He and the others, including my father, returned to our home. Servants were then dispatched to my brother's house to clean up the bloody mess that was left there.

I thank him for helping my father in the capture of the villains. He says he is glad he was able to be of service, but wishes it were not for such a dire occasion. He tells me they will be staying for a while to make sure that the uprising is over and that all the murderers are captured. I thank him for that also. It feels very unsafe to be a loyalist at this moment. It does feel good to have these soldiers protecting my family and me. With them in the castle, I know I will sleep better tonight, if I can sleep at all, that is.

I discover, in the course of our conversation, that he is a captain in the king's army and that he is from a wealthy London family. He is not a full-time soldier, but helps out occasionally, a service his family has always performed. I like this young man with the pleasant smile and calm disposition, but I am too caught up in mourning my brother's demise to care about anything else.

For days, our family suffers from the blow of my brother's death. A grand funeral follows after the usual three-day waiting period. It does nothing to ease our sorrow. It is a formality that has to be executed. We go through the motions as if we were sleep walking, only half-conscious. I continue to talk to the captain and become fonder of him each day.

Mr. Moore visits with me briefly after the funeral. We stand together under a large tree near the graveyard. "My sincere sympathy for your loss, dear friend," he says softly. "I know what you're going through. After losing my own dear daughter this last spring, I feel an emptiness in my heart and soul that is not filled by anything." As he speaks, he looks at me with tears welling up in his eyes.

"It has been so hard to accept," I reply painfully. "I keep thinking he is still here and will come walking up to see me any minute. Then I remember that he is dead. He was so much a part of my life. It's as if a part of me died with him."

"I suppose there will always be a feeling that life is no longer complete," he states resignedly, "and we will just have to go on trying to find joy in life with those who are still alive and with us now."

"You are most likely correct," I reply. "It will be hard to do, but I will try to think of my future and find happiness in my life. I know James would want me to be happy. How is your wife handling the loss?"

"Not well," he says, as tears run down his cheeks. "I am very concerned that she does not seem to be getting over the loss. Because of that, we are leaving for London permanently in autumn. Bessy and I will make a new start there. Hopefully, the newness will lighten the pain we feel at the loss of our little daughter. You can visit us there any time you like and are always welcome in our home."

He is embarrassed by the tears, but knows that I understand. "I pray you will find the peace you are seeking and that I will find something new in my life too," I say. "I don't think I shall ever be in London, but if the opportunity arises, you will be the first person I shall call upon." Tears stream down my cheeks now too.

"May we meet again along life's path. It has been my great pleasure to know you and your brother. Please feel free to call on me if you ever need anything." After a long and heartfelt hug, he departs. I stand watching as he mounts his horse and rides away, feeling a deep sadness at losing my dearest friend. My only consolation is the new friendship I have formed with Edward.

Very slowly, after a few weeks, light begins to come back into my world. At least I have someone to talk to and share my feelings with. Edward reminds me of my brother and, as James did, seems to share many of my interests. We are allowed to go out riding together, with companions of course, and to talk for hours. Gradually, I begin to look forward to seeing him each day, and often show up where I know he will be so I can see him. Being with him helps ease the pain of my great loss, and slowly, I begin to recover a bit.

Eventually though, he says he is needed in London and must return soon. I am saddened at the idea of his leaving. I do not want to face life without my brother and, now, my new-found friend. I know he feels the same as I do, but I do not expect what happens next.

OUTLANDISH IDEAS

As I speak to Edward about it, he shocks me by saying, "Then why don't you come back to London with me? You can see your dear friend Mr. Moore as well as many other interesting people. I am sure you would love London. It is such a wonderful place. My family would adore you and you would be happy there. I would be honored if you would return with me as my wife. May I have your permission to speak to your father about this?"

I am stunned. I am just beginning to recover from one huge change in my life and find myself in the midst of another possibly larger one. I don't have time to think this out; it is all so fast and unexpected. I mutter, "I need some time to think."

He replies, "There's not much time, since I leave the day after tomorrow."

"Very well," I whisper, "I will consider this and let you know soon." I feel torn. I would love to leave this castle and the limitations placed on me by being a woman in my family. There is no one left here that I feel close to. On the other hand, this is my home and my family. It is all I have ever known, and I feel secure here. The idea of leaving my home with this man I hardly know seems rash and impractical, yet exciting and fresh.

Later, as I think about it, I realize there is no longer any future here for me in Kilkenny. All that is dear to me is gone; my brother took it with him to his grave. He is gone, Mr. Moore is gone, and now I can no longer ride freely and work the birds without my brother's company. I will be confined to the castle and the grounds about it.

The thought of that terrifies me more than the idea of marrying this stranger and moving to a new home. I feel I care for him but am unsure if I love him. I am sure I can grow to love him as many women do after marrying their husbands. I think about seeing a whole new world. London is a city I have heard much about during dinners with my father's guests. It seems to me that it is a better choice to make a new start. Perhaps I will find happiness with Edward in London. I hope his family will like me, and I them.

Later that day, I meet with Edward and give him my answer. Yes, I will marry him and go to London, if my father consents, of course. He shouts for joy, picks me up, swings me around in a circle, then gently puts me down and hugs me. I look around, but fortunately, no one seems to have noticed.

The meeting with my father does not go well. We enter the room with high hopes and full of expectations about the possibilities we have discussed earlier. Edward stands tall and straight, looks my father dead in the eyes, and asks for my hand in marriage. My father glances at me then at him, sizing up the situation. Mother just sits in her chair looking as complacent as ever. I know I won't receive help from her. She will go along with whatever father says without comment, as she always does. Father rules in our household. Then he fixes his gaze on Edward.

"Were circumstances between our families of a better nature, I might be willing to consider such a merger, but they're as poor as they have always been. Your family has never gotten along well with mine, and I'll not send my daughter to them."

"We are a respected family in London, sir, and your daughter will have the finest money can buy. I pray you reconsider. Perhaps this union can help us put an end to the years of strife and misunderstanding that has come between our families."

"My daughter shall not be a peace offering or anything else to that family. I shall not reconsider it, and my word is final. If she marries you, I shall disown her, and she shall never see her family nor set foot on our properties again. She has all she needs here, and we shall find a fitting husband for her in our allies. I have no more to say to you, sir. Good day." He leaves the room abruptly. I sit there shocked and in tears. It is all over in a few seconds. All my hopes for a new life are gone. Mother, bless her heart, tries to comfort me, as does Edward.

When I calm myself, we walk together in the evening sunset. Edward is unshaken in his desire to marry me. "Come with me to England," he entreats. "You don't need your family to take care of you. I will take better care of you than they ever dreamed of. I will build you a house on a lake with flower gardens all around. It will be our house, and we will raise our own family together. Don't worry about my family; they will love you. I cannot lose you, now that I have found you. Please marry me and come to live with me in London."

THE GREAT ESCAPE

There is a long silence as I think about his proposal. Life here is certainly not going well. My brother is gone, Mr. Moore is going away, and now I am to be married off to someone I don't even know. The idea is frightening. I know I am expected to marry whomever my father decides, but I still do not cherish the idea. Here is this handsome young man offering me a new life with him.

Well, what do I have to lose? I know it is an impulsive decision, but I decide to chance that it means happiness in my future. "Yes, I will," I say breathlessly. "I will elope with you to London." Edward is delighted. His eyes dance with joy and his enthusiasm is contagious. I feel better. He takes my hand and looks deeply into my eyes. "You will never regret this; I promise you will be happy." I hope he is right. Even though I know that no one can promise happiness, I want to believe that I will find it in my new life with him.

"My father will not let me go willingly, though," I whisper, "so we will have to leave in secret. I will meet you at the crossroads just down from the castle at midnight."

"I will be waiting with great anticipation," he replies.

We walk back to the house, and I go in. My heart is flooded with all the emotions I am feeling, and my head is whirling from all these new ideas. I feel as though I were walking around in a dream. Can this be real? Am I leaving my family home where I have spent my entire life to go to some unknown place? Am I crazy or in love? What is it like to be in love? I certainly don't know. This is all so unfamiliar. Restlessness consumes me as I wait for the hours to pass until our rendezvous.

To pass the time, I pack a few things in a bag. Edward promised to buy me new clothes, so I don't take many of mine. I only take a few small treasures that are dear to me: the heart-shaped locket my brother gave me; the beautiful leather-bound *Complete Works of William Shakespeare* I received from Mr. Moore; a mother-of-pearl inlaid box my mother gave me on my 16th birthday; and hairpins of various kinds, a hairbrush, and some rose oil.

I think of my horse. If I could take her, I would feel better. Only if I did, we would be caught for sure, so it is out of the question. I look out the window and over the countryside. It is so beautiful in the pale moonlight.

How can I leave here? How can I deceive my family and go away, never to return? As I sit there waiting, I feel an inner urging to push forward with my plans; something deep inside is compelling me to do this. It feels right, though everything in my outer world opposes it. I pray to my brother in heaven to help me find the strength to do this. Immediately, a sense of calm comes over me. I feel my prayer has been answered and that my brother is with me. At least I can take him along. I am grateful for his support and feel encouraged that I am doing the right thing. Since his death, I often feel his presence and sense that he is around in spirit, watching over me.

DREAM FROM THE PAST

Finally, the hour comes. I go out my window and down the side of the castle on the trellised vines. I have done it before, but not since childhood. It seemed easier then. When I reach the ground, I walk hastily across the garden and down the hill toward town. I see the carriage hidden behind a grove of trees as I approach the road. Edward is standing there waiting with great anticipation. He hears my footsteps and looks up with an expression of relief on his face. He strides quickly to greet me. His strong arms embrace me and I feel safe at last. A wave of joy and excitement washes over me as we enter the carriage and he tells the driver to go.

We drive along all night long. I am uncomfortable and feel ill from all I have just been though. My stomach is in knots and my body aches all over. Emotionally, I am torn between the sadness of leaving my old life behind and the excitement of anticipating the new one. Here I am with a stranger going to a strange city. How could I ever have dreamed such a drastic change as this would happen to me? I think about my home. It will be a long time before I am missed because things are still awry from recent events. I often stay in my room for large parts of a day. By the time they figure it out, I will be long gone.

We reach Dublin by morning; a ship is waiting for us. We board and soon set sail across the sea for England. I am shown to a beautiful and well-appointed cabin where I lie down and fall into a deep sleep. I am so exhausted from the trip and the emotional turmoil that I sleep the entire day. As I sleep, I have a strange dream about myself living on the Isle of Man, an island just to the north of Dublin. In this dream, I am a lady-in-waiting to a great queen, a warrior queen, who is extremely beautiful. She is captured by an enemy king, who desires to marry her. But she rejects his demands of marriage. In a fit of rage, he throws the queen and all of her ladies, including me, into a snake pit. I wake up with a start. I am relieved that it was only a dream, but wonder what kind of dream that was. It seemed so real and vivid. I walk out of my cabin onto the boat's deck and stand in the wind for a while to refresh myself.

Edward comes out soon after me and we embrace, standing locked in each other's arms in the moonlight. As we stand on that deck, visions of the dream keep coming back into my mind, replaying the life with the queen and our death in the snake pit. It feels so real to me. I perceive it means something, but I don't understand what. Perhaps it is an intuitive memory of some past time. "What an unsettling and untimely dream!" I think as I stand there. Shortly thereafter, I return to my quarters and sleep for a few more hours. Fortunately this time, I sleep soundly without any further disturbing dreams. I awake feeling somewhat rested, but I am still sick in the pit of my stomach, and being on a boat for days isn't helping matters.

EDWARD'S ENGLAND

Even before I can see the lights through the clouds, I can smell the city as we sail into London. There are smells I have never known before, the smells of a big city. Then the lights of the city come into view and I am overwhelmed by the size of it. There are gas lamps lit all over. The buildings are massive and dark. It feels dirty and the smell is overpowering and worsens the closer we come to it.

I feel for a while that I want to go back to my home where everything is familiar to me. My stomach is churning by the time we land. I walk slowly off the boat and manage to get into the waiting carriage. Edward is close by my side at all times and reassures me with stories of how wonderful our new life will be. It is a long ride through London to his home, and I am not feeling as sure of my decision at this point, so I remain silent most of the time. The carriage is a comfortable one with soft seats and is fairly warm. Watching the scenery out the window, I feel happier.

We head toward the section of the city where Edward lives. Some of the city is dark and dank. It begins to smell better as we near his house, and I become more comfortable.

When we enter Edward's neighborhood, he begins telling me who lives in the houses on the way. I find it entertaining, and listen to everything he says with eager ears. There are many townhouses that sit so close together and line the streets. They are painted bright white and other sunny colors. The houses here have a lot of decorative wrought iron work, especially fences and gates. The streets are cobblestone and well kept. The many parks are green and full of roses. It is May and their scent fills the air. I begin to look forward to a new life in London.

It is quite a change from the dark stone castle I have lived in all my life. After a particularly long row of townhouses, we approach the gate of a house with a long wrought iron fence in front of a huge semicircular driveway. Their front yard is a beautifully landscaped garden. This house, unlike many others we have passed, is set back from the road a bit. The house itself is huge, not unlike Kilkenny castle. That is about the only similarity though. Unlike the castle, it is white, inviting and cheerful looking. I know Edward is from a respected family, but I have not anticipated this breathtakingly beautiful home. It is more ornate and delicately decorated than any house I have ever seen, and it is a bit intimidating.

Edward greets the gatekeeper, Tom. It is obvious from their interaction that they know and admire each other. After explaining that he is bringing home a wife from Ireland and receiving a hearty congratulation, Edward introduces me. Then we are ushered through the gate.

As we drive up to the front doors of the house, I begin to feel even more settled. They are huge double doors with shiny brass fittings, knobs, and knockers. Above the doors sits a rounded semicircular window just like the one at my house in Kilkenny. The window reminds me of home, and decreases my feeling of uneasiness. Although I am still feeling quite overwhelmed and my stomach is hurting, I like what I have seen and am feeling hopeful of my future here in London with this new family and my soon-to-be new husband. As we exit the carriage and walk up several front steps to the house, I take a second to look around. It is quite pleasant here.

We enter a large foyer after going through the front door. To my right is a drawing room with a semicircular wall. To the left is a grand staircase sweeping up. This creates the effect of standing between two half circles, one on each side. Straight in front of me is a second door that servants come out of to assist us. They greet Edward and ask if we need anything. He instructs them to bring refreshments and then he escorts me to the drawing room. In this massive room, there is a large fireplace with a wooden mantle painted white. I sit down on a long couch and look across at several chairs. All are positioned at right angles to the fireplace. It is a cozy yet splendid setting. There is a definite French influence in the decor, reminding me of pictures of the palace at Versailles.

An Afghan hound sits on the floor by the chair closest to the fireplace. He seems an amiable type and quite undisturbed by my presence. He lifts his head and observes that Edward is with me, so obviously I am a guest. He places his head back on his paws and closes his eyes, satisfied that all is well and his intervention is not required.

Edward leaves to find his parents, but soon returns, explaining that they are both out but will return shortly. He decides to show me to my room so I can rest and refresh myself. I am relieved not to be meeting his parents so soon. He is excited to introduce me, but I am so worn out and nervous. I welcome the slight reprieve.

After ascending the massive staircase with its lovely woodwork, I enter the bedroom. It is stunning, decorated gold, white, and tan with brocaded jacquard satin bed coverings and pillows. The bed is canopied and made of carved cherry wood. Several beautiful rugs cover the wood floors, and lovely windows overlook the front of the house, gardens, and, not too far off, the street. I am in the right wing of the house. The view out the window is an ever-changing kaleidoscope of people and events going on in the street. However, it is set back far enough for me to feel comfortable and insulated from it all. There is a park across the road. This scenery helps me feel more at home, since the house in which I was raised has such fine views of the surrounding countryside.

It is not long before his parents arrive. I see them from my window. His mother is plump and his father tall and large but not overweight. It frightens me just to look at him. They ask Edward to bring me to the drawing room to meet them. He comes and personally escorts me. They are nice and, of course, very polite to me, but it is clear they are not thrilled with their son's choice of a wife.

I am disappointed, but console myself with the thought that I will only have to live with them until Edward and I can build a home of our own. These are shallow, superficial people and not the kind I wish to associate with on a daily basis. Of course, I am also polite and never say a word about how I feel about them, even to Edward. He knows they're society people and he doesn't care for all that pomp and such. We agree our house will be built as quickly as possible. The idea of having my own home thrills me.

Edward introduces me to the servants. The maid and butler are very nice. He explains that he will hire a personal attendant for me so I will have someone to help me and run errands. A suitable person is soon found in a young girl, Sherry.

FROM WEDDING TO WAR

Over the next few days Edward and I keep very busy preparing for our wedding, our new home, and acquiring my new wardrobe. We see little of his parents, since they are busy with their own activities. His mother assists me when necessary, but is happy to leave most of the details to the servants and us.

We spend our days shopping for all the necessary items. It doesn't take long to discover we have similar tastes in most material things. This makes our shopping trips delightful expeditions. During this time we are spending together, I am falling more and more in love with Edward. He really is all I have ever hoped for and I feel joyous in my new-found life with him.

In the evenings, we often dine with his parents and discuss our adventures and plans for the next day's outing. One evening at dinner, while we are enjoying this pleasant conversation, one of the servants enters with a message for Edward's father. He takes it and reads it. After registering a look of complete shock, he quickly regains his composure and hastily puts the note in his pocket. Not wishing to disturb the bliss of his son's newfound happiness, he continues with the dinner conversation. I notice his reaction and wonder about it, but no one comments, so the conversation continues about daily accomplishments toward wedding and home. After dinner, Edward and I sit alone in the drawing room by the fire. Edward's father sends his servant to ask Edward to come and speak with him, so they retire to the study.

When Edward returns to the drawing room, his face is pale, and he has a wild, frightened look in his eyes. I am alarmed, since I have never seen him look this way before. He comes into the room and sits next to me on the sofa.

"I am afraid I have some bad news to share today," he says hoarsely. He takes my hand and holds it to his chest for a moment, and then lowers it and continues while still holding it tightly. He gets down on one knee and looks me in the eye as he explains, "The note my father received at dinner is a summons for my brother and I to serve in the war. It is my duty to obey, as it is part of my family obligation to do so. We should be married right away, as I must leave tomorrow. I am so sorry we cannot complete the things we planned at this time, but we will continue when I return, I promise."

"No," I state emphatically, "you cannot go. You will not return if you do. I won't let you go. Stay here with me. Remember your promises to build our house, to have children, and a happy life together. This is what is best for us." I plead with him not to go.

When he won't listen to me, I begin crying hysterically. He knows his duty binds him to this family obligation, and it is not something he can ignore without disgracing his family or letting down his country. Neither of these is he willing to do. As an honorable man, he knows he has to go and serve his country. Unable to stand my tears and pleading, and unsure what to do with this Irish outburst of emotion, he stands up, turns his back on me, and leaves the room, showing a typical British aversion to involvement in intense emotions.

Sherry tries to comfort me, but I am not a willing participant in her efforts. I cry myself to sleep that night, feeling that all is lost with Edward leaving for war in Europe.

25

NO GOODBYE FOREVER

Edward does not return to say goodbye and I cannot understand why. He leaves the house the following morning, and with his departure, all hope drains from my life. I am deeply hurt, but it does not diminish the love I feel for him and the fear I have about his endeavor.

Several days pass and they drag by so slowly it is unbearable for me. I cannot shake the feeling of impending doom. It seems palpable. Edward's parents treat me well and I never lack for anything, except sincere companionship.

Then on one fateful night, as I sleep in my beautiful gold room, I dream I am watching the war. I am flying above it. I stop on a hillside overlooking an awful scene. It looks familiar; then the memory of the horrible nightmare I dreamt the night before my brother died returns, only this time it's more real, and I know who the soldier is for whom I prayed so fervently. It is Edward.

Once again, I witness his death. Once more, life seems to drain out of me as I watch him lie still upon the battlefield. I no longer see the battle or hear the screams of death. I am screaming at God. "How can you do this to me?" I sob. "We were going to marry, and now you have taken him from me. You can't do this to me!" My heart feels heavy as I scream over and over again, "You can't do this to me! You can't do this to me! I will never see him again."

REALIZATION DAWNS

I awaken. It is very early in the morning. I am still sobbing and crying out to God when I realize that I have been dreaming. I know in my soul that this is more than an ordinary dream. Through the bed's lace canopy curtains I can see out my window. It seems surreal, as though I were not yet awake, but not asleep either. I feel as though I were in between worlds. The room is slightly lit by moonlight, and I can see the gold jacquard bedspread and the golden tasseled pillows in this beautiful room. Edward has left me here, at his home in London, to await his return. But he will not be returning. He is dead. I will never see him again.

As I stare out the window, I pray that this has only been a bad dream, but in my soul I know the truth. I have witnessed my beloved's death. As I ponder this, I perceive a dreadful, black wind rolling across the English Channel. This wind carries the message of death to all of us waiting here for our loved ones to return. I know then, as well as I know anything in my life, that this was no bad dream. It was a vision of what has taken place in a land just across the water. "No!" I cry, "No, I won't believe you!" But I know that the message this evil wind bears is true beyond any doubt. My true love is gone. I am left here alone with only my memories to ease the pain.

TRUTH REVEALED

After the initial shock, I withdraw into myself. I am numb and cannot think, speak, or even cry. My world has become all darkness and I sink into deep despair. I fall into an all-encompassing darkness with no end in sight. My life ended, along with his, on that horrible battlefield.

Days later, a courier comes with the news of Edward's death. It doesn't matter to me because I already know the truth. I have already felt the pain. It does not mean anything at all what he says now. Nothing matters anymore. Never again will I arise in the morning with a joyful heart and hopeful expectation. Never again will I look up into his loving, blue eyes. I don't care about living anymore, I just want to be with my love again, and, through his touch, find freedom from my soul-searing pain. Nothing of the material world comforts me now without my love to share it.

I remain at his parents' home in the beautiful golden room. This room, which had been my greatest delight upon my arrival in London, is now my self-made prison. His parents are devastated by the news of their son's death, but I can offer them no solace, just as they can offer me none. No one can calm my ranting or ease my sorrow. They don't know what to do with me, so they leave me where I lie in my bed. Rarely do I stray from that room.

A WAY OUT

Each day is torture from that day on. All of London is abuzz with the news of the great battle of Waterloo. The numbers of casualties are high, but the victory is great and therefore worth the sacrifice, at least to some. Napoleon is defeated and exiled. To me, the news provides little comfort; it feels like a Pyrrhic victory. Everything that is dear to me is gone, my brother, my home, and now my beloved Edward.

I cannot go home, as I am disowned, and I cannot stay here with these people who disdain me. I continue to sink into deeper and deeper states of despondency. All I can think of is that I want to be with the ones I love, and no longer have reason to remain in this world. I am stuck with these feelings and have nowhere to go. All is darkness. Lightness, laughter, and love never arise in me again.

Edward's parents, shallow as they may be, do not throw me out in the street. They have compassion for my suffering, and, in honor of their dear son, elect to keep me in their home. They have little to do with me personally, as the servants take care of everything. I am a living dead person. Each day I sink further and further down. I am hardly eating, and willing myself to die.

As the days and weeks pass, anger and hatred simmer in me and rise to a fierce boil. I am angry with God and blame him for Edward's death. Bitterness overwhelms me, and I begin to attack everyone who comes near me. The servants begin to loathe my presence, as I am so cruel to them. My maidservant,

Sherry, is particularly afflicted by my words. She says nothing, but suppresses her feelings and cowers as she fusses around the room, attending to my needs.

The cruel manner in which I treat her is beyond that which anyone can endure. She tries hard to understand my pain and ignore my constant attacks, but it wears on her until she can take no more. Under extreme duress from my continual abuse, she ends my torture with a knife. One day, she enters my room quietly and murders me with a stab in the back. The pain of the knife is small compared to the grief that my heart has contained since Edward's death. Although I am shocked to be leaving my body, that negative feeling is soon replaced by the joy and freedom of being released from my situation.

When I cross over to the other side, Edward is there waiting for me. Very shortly, we are joined by James. Although they are so happy to see me, and understand my problems on Earth, they do not give me a standing ovation for my ignoble exit from that life. I know right then and there, by the looks in their eyes, that I did not take the highest path.

Gustave Dore's Engraving from Canto V, Purgatory of Dante's *Divine Comedy*

"There are more things in heaven and Earth, Horatio, than are dreamt of in your philosophy."
– William Shakespeare, *Hamlet*

CHAPTER 2 - BETWEEN LIVES

HEAVEN, HOME AT LAST

As Edward and I move through dark space toward the light, I feel a reluctance to go on because of my recent actions on Earth. But I tell myself, "It's too late to change things now. I have to face my council and account for my actions; it's better sooner than later." How do I know I have to face a council and not God? I just know. Edward encourages me to go on toward the light, but I am feeling a resistance, a stuck feeling. I am still processing what just happened to me back on Earth. I pause for a while to collect myself. I just want to sit and sort out these emotions, but I feel the light pulling me like a magnet toward my true home.

My teacher, Kuthumi, is waiting for me at the portal of the light world. I can see him off in the distance. I realize that I've been here before, as memories of Kuthumi and the heaven world come flooding back into my awareness. Eventually, I move toward the light again and slowly begin to feel more comfortable and encouraged. The peace and love are so tangible. There is no hungry, demanding body to deal with anymore, just peace and quiet. Kuthumi welcomes me, takes my hand, and ushers me through the portal. He enlivens my energy. Joy fills my heart as I greet him. The honor and respect that I have for him is beyond measure. He has assisted me with my soul's growth for as long as I can remember. His fatherly guidance has been with me through numberless embodiments. The feeling of his familiar presence is tangible. I bathe in it for a minute. It fills me completely and lightens my soul. A moment later, I pop into that light-filled world. I am back home at last.

Heaven! I feel the light first on my face then it bathes my entire being. I am overwhelmed by the brightness. It's as blinding as sunshine reflecting off a snowy landscape. It takes me time to adjust, but I immediately feel a great sense of relief.

The feeling of safety here is tangible. I know deep inside myself that there is no danger here. I am home, safe, and nothing will harm me. Love and peace completely envelop me. It is so relaxing just to know that there are no unexpected harmful actions that I will be required to handle. On Earth, I always felt insecure because I never knew what would happen next. Even though I now know that my life was planned ahead of time, I didn't remember that when I was on Earth. It feels so good to leave all that behind. Here, in this light-filled spirit world, things are known and more predictable. It is always pleasant, fair, and consistent.

There is a luminous presence in this place that permeates everything and everyone with light. I remember now that this is my true home and light body, and I am no longer limited by the weakness of a human body and ignorance of a human mind. I now have access to vast knowledge and understanding again. The true realization of who I am unfolds in my ever-expanding mind. I know this place and all the people here. This is my home; Earth is a place I visit for a time to further my growth. I have been here in heaven for eons of Earth time. There is a welcoming feeling in the atmosphere here. It is the collective thoughts of all those souls I am connected to. I am a soldier come home from the battle, the heroine returning victorious. They applaud my efforts and welcome me home with true compassion and unconditional love.

The tests on Earth now take on a wider perspective. I no longer feel so affected by the failure at the end of my last life. That life was just one small part of my life path and development. When I am on Earth, I think my current lifetime is all there is, and I am caught up in all the drama of that experience. It becomes *the* book of my life. From this broader perspective, I now understand that *that* life was just one short chapter in a huge book of many lifetimes I have experienced, spanning more years than I can conceive of. As my awareness expands further, I realize that everyone here knows I have returned.

They are waiting to see me and discuss the experiences from my recent life. I am excited to commune with them, but there are a few things I want to do first.

HEALING TEMPLE

My first stop is the healing temple. This oblong stone facility is only one story high. It has no windows. I go here to rejuvenate and revitalize my soul after the trauma I went through on Earth, especially at my death. Here, I am able to remove the last vestiges of Earth's energy from myself. The healers in this facility shine lights of many colors on my light body as I lie floating face up above a shiny metallic bed that is curved downward, giving it depth. The bed wraps around under me and up along both sides but leaves the front of my body exposed.

The healers begin their work. They place some single-colored beams of light in specific spots on my energy body. Other places on my body are treated with several colors at once. Large lights treat a more generalized area; smaller ones treat more specific ones. Some of the light beams are flashed in sequences; others are steady. I begin to feel the remaining burdens of life on Earth lift off me. As this happens, more light and joy return to my being.

What powerful healers work here! They operate on my energy body and transform me into my true self again. I am finally free to be who I really am. The emotional overlay of the life I just left is removed, but the memory is still quite fresh. I communicate telepathically to my brother and my teacher that I am feeling better and I will see them soon. Edward has been waiting with me and observing my healing treatments. We are in bliss to be together again and beam loving feelings to each other. As I lie there basking in the light and healing, my teacher and four other master teachers appear. This is my council. They tell me that it is time for my life review. This is what I requested, since I want to get on with my learning process.

MY LIFE REVIEW

My council consists of four master teachers. They all stand facing me in a row. Saint Germain is the first to speak. He is dressed in a velvety bright purple robe with a gold metallic-looking shirt underneath, showing through in the area around his neck. His soft violet-colored eyes shine with caring and love. Around his neck, at the level of his heart, hangs a medallion in the form of a Maltese cross. The center of the cross has an amethyst that is of the deepest purple color I have ever seen. His sandy brown hair with reddish highlights along with the cut of his beard and mustache give him the regal appearance of having just stepped out of a 1700s French royal court.

The second master, El Morya, whose angular features and dark blue robe give him an intense look of someone who means business, is wearing a golden turban studded with diamonds. The largest stone, in the middle front of the turban, is a huge lapis stone, representing the will of spirit or the highest good. With his intense features and because he is extremely tall, he is somewhat imposing. Around his neck hangs a medallion with a blue stone unlike any I have seen on Earth. It is surrounded by diamonds and emits a bright white light from its center.

Kuan Yin is a pleasure to my eyes. Serving as the third master, she is a vision of beauty and moves smoothly and gracefully like a swan. Her white and violet oriental silk gown wraps around her form and drapes to the ground in layers of silky magnificence. Her hair is piled tall on her head and pinned decoratively with ornate gold and porcelain hairpins. A little gold fan-like crown sits in the front of her hair. Around her neck, at the level of her heart, hangs a crystal pendant that emanates bright white light in all directions just as a crystal, hanging in a sunny window, refracts the sunlight. On her feet are little jade-colored silk slippers.

Mother Mary, the fourth master of my council, wears a robe of many colors and several strands of opalescent pearl-like beads with hieroglyphic engravings on them. She has dark-brown, thick, slightly wavy hair worn loose and it falls just below her shoulder blades. Her olive skin is smooth and unblemished.

They all emanate feelings of deep peace, love, trust, and compassion. I am instantly comfortable in their presence. They are all the epitome of health and youth but I realize they are all ancient masters.

Saint Germain begins the review by talking telepathically about my early life and childhood, and how beautiful Kilkenny is. He asks me what I feel was good about my family and my childhood. I project scenes of my life from my memory. Everyone views them simultaneously. I observe that I enjoyed much laughter and fun times with my family, especially with my brother. I see my father, mother, older sister, my brother, and myself. I also see, with my omniscient vision, a child my parents had that was stillborn, a fact I had not known before.

Next we review my reaction to my brother's death. One of the council members, El Morya, speaks to me. I perceive no sense of judgment from him, only total compassion. "You set this situation up to help yourself learn how to handle death. Death is something that has been difficult for you in many lifetimes. Being separated from loved ones has always been difficult for you as a soul. We feel that this last lifetime was not an effective or supportive plan. We understand that you felt you could do this in that way, but we think that you were overconfident, overly optimistic. Going to Earth and expecting yourself to handle two deaths, one after the other, with little support, was not in your best interests." He stops, and Mother Mary speaks.

"You could have graduated to the next level if you had gained the understanding necessary to accept the deaths of those close to you. However, you didn't respond well, and traumatized yourself further in the process during that lifetime. This is unfortunate. We suggest you work with your teacher and your soul groups to plan a life with more support so you can gain what is needed and move on." The rest of the council indicates their agreement with her assessment by nodding.

My first response is to project a feeling of deep gratitude to them for their caring and loving advice. They project a feeling of acceptance and understanding, letting me know that they are pleased with my efforts and belief in myself.

Kuan Yin says, "We feel all is going well and you are gaining what is needed. Do you now have a clearer picture of what you will need to set up in your next life to pass to this higher level of understanding?"

"Yes I do," I reply, "and I agree with all that has been offered. I am very disappointed about not passing my test. However, I am pleased to have taken that embodiment. I learned things that will help me in the coming lifetime."

Then we review my tragic ending in that lifetime in greater detail. My last months on Earth are replayed. I experience the thoughts and feelings of everyone during that time period as if I were them. It is not something I am proud of. The review of my interactions with my maidservant is particularly troublesome. I feel the pain of her experience with me as if I were her. This definitely increases my understanding of how my actions affected her. I feel deep remorse for how I mistreated her. Even though I realize it was also a test for her, I know that I could have remained hopeful and accepting instead of rampaging against God and everyone surrounding me after

Edward's death. Perhaps then it would have been less stressful for her and she would not have killed me.

The alternate life choice is also played out for my review. I see how, if I had accepted James's and Edward's deaths, I would have gone on in that life and met another member of my family soul group, Jeff. We would have married, had several children, and I would have enjoyed a long and fairly happy life. I feel sad at the loss of that opportunity.

Next, the person from my primary or family soul group who played the role of my maidservant appears. She is one of my dearest friends here. She agreed to take on that role to be my support in passing my test. I, in turn, was giving her the opportunity to work on patience and controlling her anger. We are a great team but we failed in the last hours. She was hanged for murdering me, so her life also ends in the same time frame as mine. She will be my sister in my next life.

Fortunately, in heaven, there is mercy and understanding. Neither of us blames the other, nor are we reprimanded by the master teachers. They totally love and accept us, knowing that we have failed a difficult test but we are making progress toward our goals. They do not judge us but help us understand what is for our highest good and why. Always supportive and kind, our council members are the supreme example of what we can become. It is the exposure to their more expansive and beautiful nature that motivates me to try harder and pass my tests on Earth. I want to be like them.

They finish reviewing my life at this point. Because it is a short life and I have only one major goal, it is a short review. Sometimes this takes much longer and many subjects are reviewed in greater detail. Then they all send a message that they perceive our meeting is finished. With an acknowledgment of my divinity as a part of all that is and projecting a feeling of deep love for me as a soul, they begin to depart. I in turn send similar feelings to them as they fade from sight.

After they leave, I continue my healing process. Talking about my life is very healing because I still feel unsettled about its tragic ending. I did poorly on the last life segment. But I feel confident that the coming life will be the final one focused on this aspect of my development. That seems very good indeed.

The transformation in the healing room is near completion, and I am ready to move on to something else. I perceive the vibrations of my future stepfather, Gene. He is tickling me energetically and impressing a message in his fatherly way. "It'll all be OK kid; don't take things so seriously." Just as on Earth, my stepfather is an optimistic, merry soul.

The healers finish their work. I get up from the table and leave the transformation room. I exit the healing temple and go to the building next door, which is the place of reembodiment. I visit the life room, where souls prepare to embark for their next life on Earth.

THE PLACE OF REEMBODIMENT

The front of this cathedral-like building shoots straight up and looks like a waterfall of color falling upward to infinity. It is taller than any building I have ever seen and the top is not visible from below, so it appears to go on forever. The river of light and color that runs up the front of this building is in layers of various colors, flowing toward the top. The sparkling, shimmering patterns of opalescent blue, purple, white, pink, and indigo shades all move together in complex patterns. This is a river of constantly changing liquid light. It looks like water because it is so thick, but, in fact, it is pure light. This brightly colored liquid like substance makes up the entire front of the building. Toward the top, sparks fly out from it. I feel good just looking at it. The colors are like those in our Earth rainbow but much more intense.

Many souls preparing for embodiment sit in the preparation or briefing chairs. These resemble recliners we have on Earth, but their use is quite different. This is the place where souls get their final briefing before being sent off to Earth. Here they preview the major events that are scheduled during the lifetime to come and the goals they have made for that life. This is very exhilarating for souls, and the excitement felt in this huge room is palpable and contagious. I am bathed in it as I stand there watching the amazing process. After they finish their preview, the souls jettison up the center of the building, through the portal to Earth for rebirth and reunion with their waiting families of their soul group.

Being in the presence of souls going to Earth is an invigorating experience. They really get pumped up about starting their new lives and infect everyone around them with joy. The pervading feeling is that they can do anything. Feeling so invincible, their expectations are high.

I stand, looking earthward and watching them go up the center of the building to the portal. They look like a multitude of sparks flying out from a bonfire. Hundreds are going to Earth at a time. Each soul is aware of the others going with them and they telepathically share their excitement about what they plan to do on Earth and where on Earth they are going. It is like being in a busy kindergarten class going on a field trip. All are thrilled about taking off on their adventures.

"I am going to learn about truth," "I am going to support the world peace movement," "I am going to bring new ideas in physics," I am going to be an example of a true friend." They exclaim various things about their missions as they ascend. They have many expectations and hopes, so they are as giddy as children in an ice cream store, yet as serious as astronauts about to embark on a space mission. The possibilities seem so easy when we leave for Earth.

Having just returned from there, I try not to temper their excitement with my energy, but just enjoy the feelings generated by their positive attitudes. They are so excited about what they will do when they get to Earth. Eventually I lose sight of them as they disappear into infinite space at the top of the building, the portal to the other world: Earth

I remember what it felt like to go to Earth and the newness of that fresh experience. How exhilarating it was. I have no desire to go with them now, however. Since I have just returned, it is time for some rest and reflection.

DEVASHAN

I move on to my devashan. This is a place I create for myself. Since it can be anything I desire, I create a Hawaiian oceanfront scene with gardens coming almost to the water.

I rest here for a while on the beach. Many friends stop by. They just come and go, floating in from out of somewhere. It doesn't startle me, as it is the way we move around in this world. We think a thing, and it appears. We imagine a place, and we are there. It is all created with our minds.

My teacher, Kuthumi comes by and we discuss my next life in a little more detail. "I agree with the council's suggestion for more support. They are all delighted about your upcoming advancement," he exclaims.

I respond with, "I think I will really enjoy being at the next level because I will be able to experience and contribute more."

"You are an older soul, and this is the last test to be passed or understanding to be gained at your current level," he states, as he projects to me a feeling of what it will be like for me to exist at the next level. For a brief instant I have a glimpse of his state of being. I see that at that level, I can help more people by being in many places at one time, which is better that just bilocation; it is multilocation. My understanding is broadened and wisdom is deepened. My love is greater and can be given to many more people at one time. My mastery of emotions is incredible; only positive emotions are felt. I see that a larger percentage of my soul stays in heaven, even when embodied or appearing on Earth. I have more power to work with and accomplish assignments through well-developed psychic abilities such as telepathy, etc. I am allowed to work with even greater advanced teachers and can help Earth's evolution more. Thus I am given more important assignments.

Kuthumi's adeptship is much more expansive than what I am currently experiencing, and I love the feeling of the state of being he reveals to me. This is a teaser to encourage me to work hard to plan a lifetime that will support my gaining the understanding I need to finish my current level. There are many ways to gain the understandings for moving up levels.

From what I see in that glimpse, I know I will be able to teach more and help a larger number of younger souls gain the understandings that I have mastered. I am a teacher and healer soul, so this appeals to me. It would not necessarily be the same for other souls. We do what we enjoy doing, and healing is what I like to do most.

41

The other thing that encourages me is the feeling of love and respect I have for my teacher. I want to be like him and the others I see at the higher levels. They are so loving, caring, and compassionate.

My teacher leaves and I continue to rest and relax. I think about Kuthumi. He is a master teacher in Earth's schoolroom. My heart fills with gratitude as I think about him because of all that he has done for me, and the fact that he has volunteered to be my personal guide in this coming lifetime. He does not usually fill such a close role in my embodiments. Because Kuthumi is my teacher, other souls usually serve as my guides. They can be friends, family, or other souls in my general soul group. They are my guardian angels and help me out while I am on Earth.

My brother James visits and teases me; he has always been such a prankster. He appears in a jester outfit and asks me several riddles that all have the answer that he loves me. He is so silly. We laugh and just enjoy being together for a while. Then he goes on his merry way. He is always such a delight to work with, and a great asset to our family of souls. I spend quite a bit of time resting and basking in the beauty of the scene I have created.

SOUL GROUP MEETING

Next, I move on to a general soul group meeting where I see many of my friends. Today, we decide on a castle theme, and build it with our minds. We do this together, everyone contributing different manifestations to make it more fun and interesting. This is the large group of souls who were born at the same time I was. It is about 1,000 souls. We have been together since our birth and have always worked with each other in our lifetimes on Earth.

There are three other groups of souls I work with regularly. Two are mission groups composed of healers of various types. One has about 100 souls and the other consists of six. The third is my family group of about 100.

I arrive at my general soul group meeting and admire the beautiful castle and staging we have prepared. It is a conglomeration of the thoughts of those of us who want to participate. Our thoughtforms create it and everyone is free to add what they want to contribute to this group project. Those who have a particular need that does not fit in with the group creation simply create it for themselves to see and it is invisible to the rest of us. This allows for group and individual desires to be fulfilled.

Many souls are dressed in clothing that matches the period of Earth they lived in when castles where in vogue. It is fun to see what each person decided to wear or present themselves as. This is much like going to a costume ball. We go around and greet one another. I greet my friends Perry, Dana, Elizabeth, Dan, Paul, Christian, John, Laurence, Teresa, Frank, and many others.

This group works together to bring changes in health care on Earth. When my dearest friend Bernadette arrives, I jump into the air and meet with her. We swirl our energies around in a circular intertwining motion, spinning and dancing together. I am so happy to see her. We are the most similar in energy pattern of all the souls in my group and we reinforce each other because of that. She introduces me to a new person Joel, who is not at our level yet. His teacher suggested he visit because observing us will help him in his development, since he has similar aspirations. We greet and welcome him as an observer. The rules about observing are explained to him. He can watch everything but not hear everything. The other souls can communicate with each other and block him from hearing. This is not to be rude or selfish, but because some concepts would be confusing to him and, therefore, not beneficial.

We all sit around a large table Perry has created for us to meet. Some of the others disguise themselves as servants and pretend to serve us food at the table. Then they take off their identity blocks so we can be aware of who they are. We laugh at their antics of tricking us by cloaking themselves. It is a delightful experience enjoyed by all.

After that, we get down to the business of planning what we want to work towards on Earth. There are lots of ideas, and they are all discussed at length. Everyone is equal in his or her ability to contribute. We discuss many ideas and the implications they would have on Earth. Often, we play a "game" called futures. In this game, we thought project ideas into Earth's future and then watch the ripple effect on the planet's population as a whole. This is all probabilities, of course, but it helps us determine the best course of action.

MY FAMILY GROUP

When our meeting is finished, we all move on to other activities. I have a meeting scheduled with my family group in the library. In the wink of an eye, I am in the library, sitting down at one of the massive tables with my family soul group. I acknowledge Reva, Jeremiah (James), Clare, Michael, Alex, Shawn, Gene, Joanne, Mary (sister in last life), Clarence, Millie, Paul (Edward), Jeff, Maria, Iris, Glenn, Teresa (maidservant), Crystal, Tammy (mother in last life), Perry, Robert, Ellen, Joshua, Johanna, Timothy, and Pam.

I sit next to Paul (Edward); on his right are Clarence and Jeff. Across the table from me is Iris. Next to her on her left is Teresa and further left is Jeremiah. We sit in order of proximity to those we work with the most.

The meeting begins with a review of my last life on Earth, and then it turns to the plan for the next life. Jeremiah shows some fun scenes of ideas for our upcoming life. He offers a feeling of support to me concerning my goal. The group suggests a reinforcing energy be with me in that life to temper my emotions and keep me focused on my goals. This is a thoughtform to be created by the group, a collective intention for me to succeed in that lifetime. They pick a holographic image of me in another lifetime, as the physical reminder of this thoughtform. It is a beautiful, dark-skinned woman with long black hair. The group places their intentions into this form and decides it will be sent to overshine me while I am on Earth.

I am grateful for the group's idea and their willingness to offer some of their energy to make this hologram. It is a sacrifice on their part because they will not have access to that energy while I am using it on Earth. I understand that we are all developing together, and my progress is their progress, since we move forward, in some of our understanding and levels, as a family group. I am grateful that they are willing to do that for me. This hologram they create will constantly reinforce my life plan and assist me in staying on track. It will also reinforce my personal strengths, the best of what I embody as a soul. My lifetime is a key pivotal point in the progress of our group, so they feel sponsoring me in this way will contribute to our group's success.

As I look up while sitting at the table in the library, I feel a rush of happiness about being home with my family soul group again. I gaze up at the ceiling for a few seconds. The lights above us play beautiful patterns across the ceiling. The entire perimeter of the ceiling is surrounded at the top by sconces. The ceiling is domed, so the play of light and shadow create intricate and extremely ornate patterns.

Looking back at those seated with me, I express my agreement and gratitude to all present. We finalize who will be taking roles in the coming lifetime and who will be staying here in heaven as guides and helpers to those of us on Earth. We make a few additions to the supporting cast. After that, we chat about a few things and slowly disperse, disappearing as we move in our light bodies to our next location. I return to my devashan to think about all the topics discussed today and relax again in my beautiful retreat at the beach.

PLANNING MY NEXT LIFE

Over the course of following meetings, we add a few more reinforcing life experiences to the plan for my upcoming life: several other deaths and a birth for me to witness. I add in some career work in counseling people who have lost someone, and a passion for reading books about near-death experiences. This is such a clearly thought-out life plan, that I am confident I have all the support needed to succeed this time.

Much of my time in between my last life and the upcoming one is spent planning the details of what I will do and how I will do it. I especially plan added support and experiences that will assist me in gaining the understanding and emotional strength I will need to accomplish my goals. I feel I must pass this level not only to benefit myself but for the greatest benefit of my family soul group as well as the two larger groups.

When my plan is nearly complete, my council meets with me to discuss it. Saint Germain states, "We feel that losing your father through a divorce at an early age would be a good strategy for you. It will cause you to not be as dependent on others and, therefore, less likely to become overemotional when they leave you later in life. Less attachment occurs when you experience loss earlier in a lifetime."

After the review of the two tests regarding death that I set up in the life I just left: the death of my brother and the death of Edward, they project to me that this has been a bit of a stumbling block for me, since I still have trouble with it, even though I have worked on it for many embodiments. This last embodiment I made very little progress. They understand that I felt I could go down to earth, take a quick embodiment and pass this test, but they do not feel I was adequately prepared for something that has been so difficult for me in my past lives.

"We believe you should take a role with much more support," El Morya says.

I reply, "I agree. I knew the last plan was chancy, but I wanted to pass to the next level quickly. I really thought I was masterful enough to do it."

He continues, "You need to learn to accept the will of God, respect the life plan of the souls you are with on Earth and their cycles of return in death. You must pass this test to move on to the higher level of life experience."

I state hopefully, "We have been working on preparations for several lifetimes and one looks exceptionally promising. The plan for that life that is almost complete. My family soul group has helped me arrange many supporting events for that life. I feel it will be very successful in helping me to finally understand that death is part of the natural cycle of life and be willing to let go of those who pass on during my lifetime. We intend to reinforce that theme by allowing direct communication with my teacher and a career as a counselor that enables me to fully explore grief and loss."

My council members look clairvoyantly at the life I have been working on and agree it looks like a well-thought-out life plan with good elements of support for my learning process. El Morya says, "We feel the cast of people who are going with you for this embodiment are very well suited to their roles. The roles to be played by the supporting cast have the added benefit of helping each of them with many of the goals they're working on in their personal life plans."

They approve the embodiment our group has suggested with minor changes and additions. Although we have several possibilities for embodiments, this particular one seems very promising. My group is very excited about trying it on Earth. We have worked on several ideas for future embodiments together both in between our lives and at night when our bodies are sleeping on Earth.

Saint Germain adds, "You feel things deeply. It is a good thing, but it sometimes gets you into trouble when you become stuck in an emotional state and can't pull out of it. You love deeply and truly care for others' well-being. These are your great attributes. But you have difficulty letting go and suffer when others leave you."

They express their confidence in me and for the life I have prepared with my group. They obviously feel I will finish this lesson with this next embodiment. They show me the sign of Cancer and suggest that I be born under its influence.

El Morya says, "It will be a good influence for you since you are a very creative and emotionally expressive soul. Adding a Leo cusp would be good to temper that emotional nature. This will give you the natural tendencies needed to help you achieve your goals."

I agree wholeheartedly. "Since I am emotional by nature, being born under that astrological configuration will give me the greatest magnification of my personality."

Then they beam an image to me of a good friend of mine, named Robert. El Morya says, "He shares the same need for deepening his understanding of loss as you. We encourage you to work on a plan with Robert to support one another in the coming lifetime."

"I feel that would be helpful," I reply. They demonstrate how an arc of energy could be formed between us to strengthen both of us while on Earth. This is a fascinating technique. I have not used it before, and I am grateful to the council for their suggestion. I beam my appreciation to them.

Saint Germain has a further suggestion; "You can become close friends with Robert and then lose his friendship suddenly. Hopefully, that will help prepare you to handle larger future losses with more ease and less intense of a reaction. Remember, this is your final test on this level, and we look forward to seeing you graduate to the next one"

Before they leave, the council offers the following suggestions: "You will need to schedule the losses of two people close to you and handle them with complete understanding and love to pass on to the next level. Your mother and another close family member are our first choices for those events. The first one can be used to help you understand more and pass the second one with greater mastery of compassion and love. We feel if you can handle two deaths with understanding and emotional stability, you will have done enough to pass."

The council suggests that we schedule the death of one family member when I am young so that I can learn about death early in my life while my intuitive mind is still very active and I have not yet been influenced by the current belief systems of Earth regarding death. I project my agreement and profound gratitude for their wise guidance. Their confidence in me gives me a great boost of confidence in myself. I am sure I will succeed this next time.

PREPARING FOR REEMBODIMENT

In my family group, we plan the two deaths suggested by our council as well as several other life experiences to deepen my understanding of loss. After many Earth years have passed, all seems as ready as it could possibly be, so I prepare myself to reembody. Several family members and supporting characters in our little group, including my father and mother in the life to come, have already embodied. My time approaches swiftly, and I am eager to join my groups on Earth to enact our plans, especially my family group.

I feel a tugging at my energy urging me to start the next cycle of Earth incarnation. Those who work in the reembodiment center know of my decision to return to Earth. I feel myself in the recliner of the briefing room in the reembodiment building. The attendants begin by showing me the children I will have on Earth and what wonderful souls they are, how we will help each other, and the experiences we will share. My attention is held on that idea for a while, but my resistance mounts as I approach my imminent return to Earth. My thoughts turn away from it to my mission group and the fun we have together here. That thought takes me immediately to be with my friends here again. I am with my group and we talk about the fun we are going to have on Earth together and the goals we are planning to implement in this coming lifetime. I am excited about that and about my well-planned-out lifetime. All that planning, plus the reinforcement of my group through the overlay hologram, as well as the mission group's plans are all great reasons to get going. Much good will come to individuals and to the planet if we accomplish all that we have planned.

MY MISSION GROUPS

Within the general soul groups there are smaller groups of souls called mission groups. Just like it sounds, these are souls who come to Earth with a certain mission to fulfill together or have a similar path in life.

In addition to the studies with my general soul group and individual training with my teacher, I also meet for a period each day with my doctors' mission group (about five souls) and less frequently with my healers mission group (about 100 souls) for this upcoming life. When I meet in my doctors' mission group, there are usually five of us, but a sixth one will occasionally attend. He is an understudy, sort of a backup. Should any of us fail to fulfill our life plan by getting distracted and forgetting what we were supposed to do, he will step in and replace that one. He will embody at the same time as we do in case he is needed. The members of my group are John, Dan, Laurence, Allan, me, and the alternate Thomas.

The souls in my mission groups are all healers. We have all been healers in many lives and have tremendous knowledge in that area. We have been together before in past lives, bringing advanced methods of healing to Earth. I can remember what we did in several of those embodiments.

Both of my mission groups are very forward-thinking groups. We are all strong souls who don't care much about what others think of the ideas we bring to Earth. The groups envision the effect our contribution can make on the future of health care in that world. I am to spearhead some ideas, but it is a collaborative effort. We want to see more energetic medicine used on Earth. As a result of our work, we hope that people will understand healing in a different way. We also want to implement a new health care model. Disease will not be as important on Earth after we are there this time. My general soul group will support us in various ways. My good friend Dana is with me and we talk about the ideas we both have for accomplishing that goal. I am getting more excited about going back to Earth now, but still feel some resistance.

My dearest friend Bernadette joins us and reminds me that we'll be together in this coming lifetime and mirror each other's lives. We set this up to help each other by providing validation that we are doing what we planned.

"Remember you can just call on me anytime. If we are doing the same thing, we will know we are on track. It will be so much fun!" she exclaims enthusiastically.

"I feel like a kid who's reluctant to go to summer camp," I reply.

MY HEALING WORK IN HEAVEN

I think of my work here in the heaven world. When people are injured by a trauma, especially at death, I help them heal. I perform that healing in the receiving room. This is where souls come when they first arrive from Earth. If they have had a traumatic death that involved being tortured, raped, or murdered, especially if they were young, inexperienced souls and did not pull up out of the body before death, then their energy is damaged by that trauma. My job is to heal that negative effect so they can feel light and be joyous again. They lie floating above the metal table in the room. Standing about five feet from them, I take different frequencies and colors of light, and use them to remove the blockages and repair the damages to their energy bodies.

Sometimes I use a glowworm-like oblong mass of concentrated liquid light to heal extremely damaged areas. I work from the top of their head, then usually off to one side or the other, depending on where the damage is. I am very skillful at this. When I finish with them, people are very grateful to feel like their old selves again. I think about all the embodiments I have had as a doctor and healer; there have been many. In this world, I teach many doctors and healers. On Earth, I will not be a doctor this time. I am concentrating on having a family with a husband and children, and passing the test I didn't pass the last lifetime.

It has been 141 Earth years since I came from that last life, but time is so fluid here, it seems like yesterday. I begin to move my energy toward the reembodiment room. As I do, I move past an area that I dearly love here in the heaven world. It is a place of inspiration. In these tall, majestic buildings are individual meditation rooms. Souls love to visit these rooms where they put themselves into a deep meditative state to receive inspiration and ideas from the universal energy. A soul in that state can tap into the collective mind, which is like a giant computer bank of knowledge. Infinite possibilities are experienced in this place. A soul can go there with the intention of knowing about a certain subject or just go for general ideas. The ideas received here may never have been discovered before. It is an inductive or prepared environment, similar to a Montessori classroom on Earth. I love these buildings. They are very tall and have three sides, forming a triangular shape. They slope seamlessly to the top, which is pointed. The sides of these particular buildings are slick and shiny. They look like they grow right out of the ground. I want to go in but I simply admire them as I pass by.

Next, I pass the magnificent Grecian gardens where lovely flowers of all shapes and colors exist in perfect balance along with fountains and columns. This place reminds me of ancient Greece on Earth. The fountains, however, can flow in any direction and there are other, more innovative, water features in these gardens than I ever saw in Greece. It is a great place to bask in beauty and relax for a time. There is a group of students here today learning the art of creating flowers. I watch for a while, observing their efforts. It is a small group of only five. Most of them are just beginning to get the concept and can only make a petal. I just finished my lessons on flowers and have moved on to creating trees, so I am familiar with what they are trying to do. I lend my energy through supportive thoughts and understanding, giving them access to my knowledge of this art. This helps them. They must draw and focus enough energy to form the entire flower for it to manifest. Yet they cannot try too hard or it doesn't work. It is more like feeling it done already and holding it gently while the energy flows into and fills up the thoughtform.

It takes much concentration and ability to gather and hold the energy long enough to completely form the flower. The colors of flowers they are making are the most beautiful shades of lavender, sea foam green, and peach. They look almost fragile; they are so delicate and paper-thin.

COMMUNICATION

I am familiar with their teacher, so we talk telepathically on a frequency the students cannot tune into. Our private conversation is not an affront to the students, as they "hear" at their level, and, as they develop, they naturally hear at more advanced levels. They know they don't hear above their level because they would not understand the communications on this level. They do not feel slighted, but look forward to attaining the next level of understanding.

This form of communication by telepathy is much better and understandable than talking. It is the primary form of communication in heaven. It is more of a whole form, allowing the entire concept to be given with the intention, feeling and motivation. There is much less miscommunication this way. Lying is not possible, since all is known and truth is evident. No one would even attempt to lie because it is not possible to get away with that here. After a long thoughtful stroll, I decide it is time to get going and prepare for my reembodiment on Earth.

I go for an energy bath to clear my energy and align myself for my coming journey. I enter a spa-like enclosure that is a wind tunnel energy bath. It is invigorating, much like a massage or a whirlpool bath. It is used for refreshment like tea-time or ice cream on Earth. It is something we do just for enjoyment.

ANIMALS

As I think about life on Earth I remember how much we enjoy animals that live there. I look forward to interacting with those loving beings again. On Earth, we have animals that give us unconditional love. In heaven, we are all giving that to one another all the time, so we don't need animals. Animals do not exist in the heaven world, as we know them on Earth. They are a separate evolution that coexist with us on Earth, a different life form. When they die, they return to the energy from which they came, and are made into another animal, which can even return to interact with the same people repeatedly. They retain their own energy, but they are more like a huge conglomerate soul. We co-inhabit this planet with them and get along quite well, but we are not from the same place.

In heaven, I can see where the energy that was a certain animal I had as a pet is currently residing and how it has evolved since it left us last. I can also recreate the pet. This is just for my enjoyment and that of other souls I embodied with. It is not a permanent item, but just a hologram of the original being.

ANGELS

I think of how I will change once I return to Earth and have a body again. How my understanding of the way everything works in heaven and Earth will become blurred again. Reality will not be easy to understand. I remember the many misconceptions about heaven that exist on Earth and how I will be blind to the truth again when I embody. I begin thinking about the various misunderstandings such as sin, hell, death, and heaven.

Angels are one big misunderstood topic on Earth. I have never seen anyone here with wings. No one sits around playing harps either. We do see them on earth though. The angels many people feel and see on earth are oftentimes their guides, teachers, family, or soul group members. Some are helper souls that have chosen that job in heaven; they are all labeled angels when they visit earth. Because heavenly visitors are in a different vibratory frequency, when they come to Earth to help people, they are often seen as having wings. I think this may be because they are beings of light, and that energy glows around them as an aura of great power and brilliance. Their "wings" are sometimes the representation of that light of the heaven world and its vibration. Even I have been mistaken for an angel when doing healing work on people. Also, guides and loved ones can appear in any form that is comforting for the person they are helping, so they can appear with wings if that is a form that is easiest for the person to understand and work with. There may be winged angels in another part of the universe. I have never seen them here but I am sure grateful we have such helpers when I am on earth. I love my "angels" whoever they are, with wings or not.

RETURN TO EARTH

I finish my musings about Earth and its misinterpretations of heavenly messengers, and begin to come to terms with the fact that it is time for me to return there. The pull to the chair is feeling stronger and I know it is time to return. The reason it has been 141 years since I was on Earth is because I had to wait for certain soul group members to be on the same embodiment cycles to go with me into this lifetime. The time has come, and I am eager to join my team. I still feel reluctant about leaving the beauty and grace of the heaven world, but that feeling is now overridden by my desire to accomplish the goals I have made for the lifetime to come. It is very exciting. As soon as my thoughts go there, I am back in the briefing room chair. I have already decided how much of my soul essence will be going to Earth and how much I will leave in heaven. It is a 60/40 split. I decide to take the majority of my energy to Earth to make sure I have enough to accomplish my intended goals. The rest of my energy will remain in heaven with my soul groups. It is normal to bilocate. In this way, we are always together, even when some of us embody. Separateness is an illusion that only happens on Earth because, in heaven, we are always with those who we are close to.

My dearest friend and teacher Elizabeth arrives to wish me well on my journey to Earth. She is radiantly beautiful and her light is very bright. Kuthumi arrives and we preview scenes from my upcoming life. Scenes of my children, my husband, and of me working toward my goal alone, and with my group, flash quickly before me. I am reminded of changes we will enact on Earth and the major tests I need to pass. I now feel ready and excited to return to Earth. That feeling draws me upward into the reembodiment tunnel. I am with many other souls who are also going to Earth. We are all so excited. The atmosphere is one of a bus full of kids on a field trip. I am not as excited as some souls, who are almost giddy with anticipation. They are really pumped up about it. I am excited about having my children, husband, and changing medicine.

The pull through the tunnel is now very intense and I could not turn back if I wanted to. I repeat over and over to myself the affirmation, "It's going to be good, it's going to be good, it's going to be good!" It gives me a comforting feeling. The energy is pulling and pulling. I can see Earth at the end of the tunnel and continue to be drawn toward it. It comes more into focus as I move closer to it, much like an astronaut moves toward Earth from space. What an awesome, beautiful planet Earth is. I admire it as I rush toward it at light speed.

I arrive just over the city of Los Angeles where I will be born. The first thing I do is check out the baby body I will inhabit. It is in the beginning of the second trimester, so I have some time before I have to embody. There are many other souls who have arrived and are not going into their bodies full time yet. We visit places together on Earth that we loved when we were here before, and we enjoy some wonderful memories from those times. We hang around together until our time comes. I don't cherish the idea of putting on a body because it is heavy and restricting and has numerous needs and desires.

PREPARING THE BABY BODY

Eventually, I go into the body of the baby I will be integrating with and begin the process of preparation for our lifetime together. I experience a sucking and a cramped, genie-in-the-bottle feeling as I enter that little space. When I am settled, I begin to check out the body. Like a pilot checking out my plane before takeoff, I activate systems and organs that are not working at full capacity. I am at the control center where I review all of this body's structure, development, and functions. If there is anything wrong at this point, I can fix it with my ener-

57

gy, but not if it is an illness or disability needed for what I have written into my plan for this life or my parents' plan. We are integrating; we sort of meld together, becoming a whole human being. Everything proceeds without any problems. We are a good team, my new body and I, but it still feels so uncomfortable to be in a body. I leave the baby body periodically in the next few months, especially when it's sleeping. I love the expansive feeling of being out of the body in my soul form and traveling around Earth.

My day finally arrives, July 20, 1956 in St. Francis Hospital, Lynnwood, California. It is time for me to be born. It is nearly noon, and I feel a great pressure on the body as I slip through the birth canal to the open air of the room. It is cold, bright, and noisy. Every one of my senses is on fire from the overload of sensory input. I scream silently, and then begin breathing. Even that hurts, since these lungs have never been used before in the open air. Fortunately I don't have to be slapped on the bottom, since I come out breathing already. So I am saved one more insult to my already stressed body.

The doctor puts me on my mother's tummy. It is so warm and soothing and I feel some comfort and safety. But then, they pick me up and begin checking, poking, and messing with me. Finally, they wrap me in warm blankets and return me to my mother, where I feel secure and loved again. The veil of forgetfulness descends over me as I begin my new life on Earth. Slowly, memories of the other world become vague thoughts and dreams. Eventually, I am fully integrated with my new self, and memory of the heaven world no longer guides me.

CHAPTER THREE - LIFE BEGINS AGAIN: CHILDHOOD MEMORIES

MY SISTER MARY 'S REBIRTH

As I settle into my new life, I become more and more unconscious. The memories of who I am, what I have come to Earth to do, and my great plans for this lifetime begin to fade. Occasionally, I have memories of heaven, especially when I am sleeping, but they seem like dreams. Each day, I forget more and more who I really am and enter fully the life I am now experiencing.

My first major event in this lifetime is the birth of my sister, Mary Louise in a hospital in Portland, Oregon. It is an exciting time for our family. However, her time with us will be short.

On the day she is three months old, our parents need to pick up something from their friends, so they stop by their house. It's a freezing winter day and our father, Shawn doesn't want to take us in with them. "Just leave them in the car where it's warm," he says. "We'll only be gone for a few minutes. Quit worrying, they'll be fine."

"I just don't like to leave them alone," JoAn, our mother, replies. "Just come on; they're waiting for us," Shawn retorts in a pushy tone. Rather than risk a chill on this bitterly cold day, they leave us in the warm car while they go in to take care of business. They were only gone a "few minutes."

Mary is asleep in the bassinet beside me on the back seat. The bassinet is covered over with a blanket. I am sleeping too, but I wake up and become aware that something is happening with Mary. As I watch, her soul lifts out of her body and the bassinet. She is in her light body. I wonder what she is doing. She hovers above the bassinet for a while and speaks to me telepathically.

"That body is too sick," she says to me as her soul slips out of her dead body. She is very calm and continues gently, "I have to leave now, but I'll be back with you soon; I have to get a new body." Although she is just an infant, she is fully aware and can communicate with me easily. I understand her perfectly. Actually, I understand her much better when she is out of her body than when she was in it. I know she will be near in spirit, but am concerned she is leaving me physically. She senses my apprehension and sends me comforting feelings. "Everything will be fine," she reassures me as she leaves. Her departure feels very natural to me.

Mom had been quite chilled as she walked from the car to the house, so she warmed herself by the wood stove for a minute. As she stood there, a feeling of dread passed through her. Her mind flashed on Mary for a second, but she reminded herself that Mary was fine and sleeping peacefully, so she dismissed it as a passing fear.

When my parents return to the car, they think Mary is still sleeping, so they do not uncover her. Arriving at home, Dad puts the heat on to warm the house. They leave Mary's bassinet covered. When the house warms up, Dad goes over and lifts the blanket. Mom knows, by the pale, shocked look on Dad's face, that something is terribly wrong. She feels in her heart that Mary is dead before she even sees her. At that moment, she knows the reason for her earlier feeling of dread.

As my father begins administering resuscitation, Mom calls the ambulance, hoping that somehow, someway her baby could be saved. She knows, deep down, that they're only going through the motions because the baby was already gone. Mary is blue and she is not breathing. I watch calmly with my sister who has returned in her spirit body and hovers there beside me. "They'll be OK," she whispers. "I'll be back soon." She moves closer to my mom, comforting her, and then fades from my sight. I still feel her presence with me even though she is "gone."

At the hospital, Mary's body is pronounced dead on arrival. Mom is shocked, staring at the body of her baby in disbelief. She says, "How can this be? Only a few hours ago she was fine, and very much alive."

Later, my parents are even more shocked to find out that the hospital had a bacterial outbreak and most babies born in that hospital at this time die. The doctors call it "sudden infant crib death," caused by a staph infection whereby the babies' lungs fill up with fluid and they just stop breathing. They say it is a very painless way to go, which explains why my sister was so quiet and peaceful about it. The hospital remedies the problem, but not in time for my sister.

MARY'S RETURN

Life goes on and Mom soon becomes pregnant with another child. It is Mary again. I know because I talk to her soul as it hovers around my mother. I don't feel the loss of my sister because she is always around us in spirit. Mary comforts my mother and father for a long time. She comes and goes in her spirit body as souls often do when they are waiting to be born. Just before she is born she is almost always in the body of the new baby.

My mother refuses to go to the hospital to have her baby because of her previous experience. She gives birth in the doctor's office instead. In the confusion, everyone forgets about me, so I am present in the room for my sister's rebirth. I am there to welcome her back to our family and physical life.

The baby comes out screaming. My mom is happy to know she is a healthy, live, and breathing baby girl. She names her Teresa Louise. Teresa/Mary still picks a very unhealthy body, but at least she stays alive this time.

61

Although grateful for Teresa, my parents suffer for many years, thinking they have lost Mary forever. I think, "If only I could tell them what I saw, they would understand that she is fine, and her soul never totally left; in fact, she's still here." It would help ease the pain of losing her physically. Nothing can completely take away the pain of losing a child, but an understanding of Mary's reincarnation can make it more bearable for them.

This is the first experience I have with death and reincarnation in this lifetime. My second experience occurs at my grandfather's funeral. I am about nine at the time.

MY GRANDFATHER'S FUNERAL

My mother, Teresa, and I arrive at the church in Eugene Oregon on a clear, sunny Sunday afternoon. As the funeral begins, people start crying and wailing about my poor grandfather and how he is suffering so much because he's in hell.

I ask Mom, "Why are these people crying, and why do they think grandpa is in hell?"

"I will tell you later; be quiet now," my mother replies.

I am very confused. Grandpa, in his light body, is standing right here in the room with us. He looks fine and appears to be quite happy. I don't understand why everyone thinks he is having some kind of problem. I know that his physical body is dead, but in his light body, he looks better and seems happier than I have ever seen him.

He doesn't interact with me as my sister did, but he is aware of me and knows I can see him. He probably doesn't speak to me because we didn't know each other well when he was alive. He is busy watching his own funeral proceedings.

I finally realize that people are crying because they can't see him. They think they have lost him and that he is gone to hell. They also have some crazy idea that because he is not a

Christian, he will not go to heaven. I know better. I don't know why, but that does not sound true to me. He has probably already been to heaven and is just back here for a visit. Why don't they understand that he's alive and well? He's right here in the room. It is so obvious to me. He'll be reborn into a body again, just like my sister; he just has to go get a new one.

Even though I have never heard the words "reincarnation" or "soul," after these two experiences, I feel they are just a natural part of life. I never think about there being any other possibility. The second experience does leave me wondering why people don't know about these things that seem so obvious to me.

THE BAPTISM

My first experience with the heaven world in this lifetime occurs when I am 11 years old. We attend a small church in Fall Creek, Oregon. The minister is one of those special souls who seem to walk and talk with God continually. I think that he knows God personally. His sermons are such loving, Holy-Spirit-filled communications. One Sunday in June, the minister asks if I want to be baptized. I think this over and decide it is something I want to do.

The day of the baptism is a balmy summer day. We don our white gowns and walk to the creek where the minister waits to perform the ceremony. In our bright white robes, we seem to be glowing as the sunlight hits us, making us appear as if we were lit from within. We look like a band of angels descending from heaven as we walk in procession, down the hill toward the spot where we are to wait our turn. The only things missing are our wings. Our appearance contrasts sharply with the blanket of green trees behind us, creating a very ethereal effect. It is as if we were witnessing a heavenly event.

We wade to where the water is about waist deep. One by one, we proceed to be baptized. The minister prays over each of us in turn. My mother goes just before me. I watch as our minister lays her backwards until she is completely sub-merged. Even her face is under the water. Then it's my turn. Someone announces my name, "Tonya Marie Hudelson." I walk further out into the cold, but somewhat refreshing water.

As the minister's words, "In the name of the Father and of the Son and of the Holy Spirit, I baptize thee…" reverberate in my ears, he tilts me slowly backwards. The cold water floods over me and puts my body into shock. Then my face goes under, and the real awakening begins. Something in that experience wakens me spiritually. Normally, the cold water going over my face would have frightened me, but I am trans-fixed. It feels like time stands still and I am frozen in some al-tered state of consciousness.

I feel a peaceful and loving presence with me that is familiar to me. I have a flash of myself in a lighter, freer, spirit body. Then a tender, caring feeling washes over me. I am in communion with the heaven world for an eternal moment. I touch something profoundly wondrous and beautiful, even if this touch is only for a second. I want more of that kind, soft, loving feeling. I just want to stay here forever. It feels like I have come home to those who know and love me for who I re-ally am. This feeling buoys me up and gives me a deep sense of support and unconditional love.

This revelation is over in a flash, and in the next instant, I become acutely aware of my body. This startles me, and I jump up out of the minister's arms, as those watching gasp. What I am aware of most in that moment is my grandmother's face. She is standing with others far away on the opposite shore, watching the baptism. When I jump up, her face is in sharp focus close before me. It is full of pain, from a memory too painful for her to recall consciously. I can actually feel her pain, although I do not understand what it is from. It is as if I were one with her for a moment, with her and everything else all at once. Then, in another instant, I am back in my body again. The minister helps me steady myself, and I wade to where the others stand on the bank of the creek. I feel different, somehow altered from my former self.

From that day on, I feel a loving presence with me wherever I go. I call the presence "God" because that is all I know it can be. I know his voice and I know there is much more to life than what I can see with my physical eyes. There is another beautiful, unseen world inhabited by invisible beings. I glimpsed that world and felt its peace, even if only for an instant. I want to go back there to feel that incredible peace again.

I know my life is going to change from this day on *and change it does*...

MEETING "THEM"

This guiding presence I call "God" becomes my best friend and constant companion. I ask him questions all day long about various things and he explains them to me. It is a wonderful relationship. I am known for being an extremely happy child, and this relationship of constant communication with spirit is the reason. It is a great way to live.

Many of my best childhood memories are of riding my bike around our neighborhood while having many wonderful conversations with "God."

My sister Teresa and I are also aware of a group of beings we call "them." "They" come into our lives at about the same time as the God presence.

"They're here. Do you feel them?" Teresa asks, looking up at me, where I am sitting on the steps of our back porch.

"Yes, I do," I reply. "What were we talking about just before they came? Oh yeah, you were talking about angels. That's one of the things they like. Boy, they sure feel close today."

"I wonder what they are." Teresa says, looking around.

"They don't feel like ghosts or anything bad. Maybe they're angels," I venture.

She gets up from the grass and comes to sit beside me on the steps. It feels better being side by side when we are sensing "them" even though we feel perfectly safe. They seem very loving and kind. Judging from their favorite topics, we feel they are good spirits, whoever "they" are.

"Why do they always come so close when we talk about angels, God, heaven, or revolution?" Teresa asks thoughtfully.

"I don't know," I reply, "but they sure do make it clear what they're interested in, don't they? Every time we talk about regular things like our family or what's happening today they just go away."

We pause for a moment and just feel them. It seems as if they were right next to us and that there were two or three of them. We remain silent for a few moments, both of us tuning into "them."

"I wonder why they come to us," I say finally. "They don't seem to be around other people. Grandma, Grandpa, and Mom don't feel them, and I've never heard anyone else talk about them."

Teresa replies, "I know and I don't bother to ask the grownups because they always say to stop imagining things. Do you think they're in our imagination?"

"No, I don't," I answer, looking longingly at the creek in back of the house. "Well, let's go play in the creek. Maybe we can catch a few crawdads before Mom calls us in for dinner."

"OK," she says, "that sounds like fun."

I jump off the stairs and head for the creek, scanning the area for a container to put our "treasures" in after we catch them.

Although my sister can see auras, she seems to know no more about "them" than I do. They are our greatest mystery, and we love having a secret no one else knows about. We know, from reactions we have received previously, that invisible friends are not something to tell grownups about. They don't believe in them, and it isn't worth trying to convince them. We spend many summer days, sitting by the creek in back of our house, trying different subjects to see if they would come closer or go further away. My sister and I often discuss that we have come to be a part of a revolution on Earth. We feel it will be a positive revolution, like a change in people's ideas and beliefs, not a bloody mess like some of Earth's past revolutions.

It feels more like a revolution in consciousness, an awakening of some sort. They communicate to us that to be a part of this time in Earth's history is a great blessing. I think the process of communing with these beings is getting me ready for the next big step in my life of meeting my spiritual teacher.

MY FAMILY

My family consists of my mother JoAn, my father Shawn, stepfather Gene, sisters Teresa and Tamara, and half-brother Timothy. Teresa and I get along well and spend most of our time together. She is my best friend. We share the same interests, the main one being spirituality. The two younger children in our family, Tamara and Tim, form a second group. They are not interested in the "unusual" things Teresa and I are fascinated with. They spend more time with each other and with their friends. Teresa and I have a loving relationship most of the time, although we have two things we have brought over from our last life together that are a recurring problem. I love

67

to torment her and tease her, and especially love to call her names. Her reaction to that is to become furious and hit me. Twice she tried to stab me with a knife from the kitchen.

My father, Shawn, is a normal American guy who works for the phone company, plays country western music professionally, and owns a restaurant. Mom sings in the band and runs the restaurant. She also takes care of us, of course.

Childhood isn't what I would call easy. We suffer years of physical and emotional abuse from my father, who is an alcoholic. Alcohol eventually ruins his ability to function effectively in life, and when I am 6, my father runs off with the other singer in their band, and my parents divorce.

Our "second life" with Gene and his family is quite different, since they are a loving and wealthy family. I am showered with all the love and attention I need as well as all the material things I could ever desire. They own several phone companies, a lumberyard, and a grocery store.

One of my fondest memories of this time is playing with the old-fashioned phone switchboard my stepfather brings home for us. We spend hours sitting with our headsets on pretending that we are operators connecting calls with long colorful cords that we plug into slots. We disconnect the calls by pulling the cords out rapidly one after the other and squealing with delight as they retract automatically into their receptacles.

When I am 10, my mother decides to divorce Gene and raise us by herself. She feels she doesn't really love him. I am not sure she really knows what love is. I sure like Gene and his family. But I respect her choice and am very proud of her when she decides to go to college two years later to earn her degree in education. She works day and night toward this goal.

While she struggles through college for seven years, I am left to raise the younger kids. This puts a lot of pressure on me. Mom is gone most of the time either at work or school. Those are hard years, but a lot of growth comes out of them. It teaches me about being responsible for others and how to sacrifice for the common good. It is a lot of work. Many people do not understand my life.

TERESA AND HER AURAS

My sister, Teresa, is the closest to me in age and is my dearest friend and confidant. We share many adventures and, because of a mutual interest in spiritual things, spend many days and nights talking about our unusual experiences and ideas.

Many people are born with gifts. My sister has the gift of being able to see the light field or aura that exists around people and around just about everything else. It is not visible to most people, but she always sees it. It consists of many colors.

"Do you think he's strange?" I ask Teresa about a man we just met at the store."

"He has very dark colors around him," she replies.

We get in the very back of the Mercury station wagon and sit next to each other so we can continue the conversation without my mom, who is driving, overhearing.

"Do you always see light or color around people?" I whisper.

"Always." She pauses thoughtfully for a minute, and then begins describing a world I have never seen. "I see lights around everyone, some are beautiful and bright, but others are dark and muddy. The beautiful ones are around nice people who are doing good things. They look like the rainbows you see around lights after you've been swimming. The dark ones are around those who are doing bad things and hurting people. They look like dirty dishwater. Many people have both light and dark colors, but usually more of one kind. Each color tells me something about them."

"Do the dark ones scare you?" I ask.

"Sometimes, if they're very dark, but I haven't seen very many of those," she answers.

"What does it look like when you see all those lights?" I inquire.

"Most of it is very beautiful. It looks like everything around is in a beautiful bubble of rainbow colors. The people, the trees, the animals, they all have light around them. When they touch each other, the light can go from one thing to another. Like when a person pets a dog, the dog gives out loving colored light. This light goes into the person and makes their auras even brighter.

"I want to see someone bite an apple while it's still on the tree so I can see the light from the tree go right into the person. Once the apple is picked, its light begins to go down, so it doesn't give as much energy to the person. Live things have the most energy, especially people, but everything has energy around it. When I look at the world I see all kinds and colors of lights."

We arrive home and go to sit on the steps in the backyard, our favorite place to talk like this. "Look at the creek," says Teresa. "See the light on it? That's a clear light; the trees have it too, but they also have a green light. Jake [our dog] has a lot of good energy around him because he's happy and healthy. He has a yellow light.

"Some people have energy that goes way out from them. Their light is bright. They help people and are very kind. Selfish, mean people have light that is close around them. Their light is dull. The really special people have a huge amount of bright white light around their head like the picture of Jesus at church. The more good things people do, the more beautiful is the light they have around them."

I think about this world of hers for a while as I sit bathing in the sunlight. It sounded wonderful. "Do you like seeing all those beautiful things?" I ask her.

70

"Well, I do like those, but the dark things are scary sometimes," she replies.

"I don't like the bad people either. Can you tell if someone is lying or cheating?" I ask.

"Yes I can, but I try to love them anyway. They have to learn for themselves that it's better for them to do right things," she answers.

"I've always wondered about that because you give people way more chances than I do. I can feel if they have bad energy and I just stay away from them. You always go along with them anyway. Aren't you afraid you'll get hurt?"

"No, I'm not because I can tell by their colors if it's OK or not. I stay away from the really bad ones."

"Do you think it will ever go away and you'll be like a regular person?"

"I don't know, but sometimes I wish it would."

We stop talking and I think about what she says for a long time afterward, especially about what life looks like to her.

"All learning here is for the highest good and spiritual development of each soul, just as it is on Earth." - Kuthumi

CHAPTER FOUR - MEETING MY TEACHER
KUTHUMI

THE KEY TO THE LIGHT WORLD: HOLDING THE POINT

When I am eleven, we live in a small house on a creek, close to my grandparents. My bedroom is a small room with a nice little loft. When our nanny comes to live with us, she is given my bedroom and I am moved to the loft. At first I am angry about losing my bedroom to this intruder, but eventually I begin to like being up and away from everyone else in the house. Especially my younger siblings, who like to get into everything I own on a regular basis. I enjoy this new level of privacy, and begin spending more and more time in my little nest.

The entire space is about the size of a king size bed and I have to climb a ladder to get there, but I love it. This is my personal retreat from the world. The presence of "God" is with me everywhere, but always feels closer to me there.

One day after school, I crawl into my little loft and I lie down on my bed. As I lie there, the God presence speaks to me as it has been doing for months, ever since my baptism. The feeling of deep love and concern I always feel from this presence is tangible. I feel safe, loved, and happy. The love emanating from this presence penetrates every cell of my being. Joy fills my heart as I begin my daily communion with it.

This day, in my loft, I am lying quietly on my bed, looking out the window at the peaceful green of the forest. My little twin mattress is parallel with the top window, so I can see the creek at the back of our house. I am just lying there looking at that beautiful view. As I close my eyes, I imagine the wind blowing through the trees and across the grass in the field and the water running swiftly in the creek outside my window.

As I lie there, I have a strong feeling to try and hold the point of restful alertness between waking and sleeping, that minute point just before falling asleep. The whole concept of holding that point is just put into my mind by the God presence. I feel as if I have always known how to do this, even though I have never done it in this life. Each time I feel myself slipping toward sleep, I remind myself to focus my mind on that point and try with all my will to stay on that spot. This is the hardest thing I have ever tried to do in my life; it takes every ounce of my energy to keep my mind focused on that place. While I am on that point, I begin to notice a transition is taking place.

As I gradually slow down my wandering thoughts and eventually stop them, a sense of incredible peace and tranquility envelops my entire being. I feel at one with everything, God, the universe, all of life. I no longer feel like a separate being. I am aware of myself, but as a part of a larger whole, like I am connected to all life. I am part of all that is and I am floating in a sea of oneness. It feels so wonderful, that I just want to stay there forever.

Each day after that, when I get home from school, I practice holding "the point." At first, it is very difficult to maintain the level of concentration needed to do it. I struggle to maintain it for longer periods of time. With intense mental focus and much practice, I am eventually able to stay there and hold it for as long as I want. I also practice at night as I am falling asleep.

In the morning, I try really hard not to move or think when I awake. I want to just hold that point so I can once again feel the rush of peace and tranquility. It does not feel like a wide point; it feels like I am trying to focus my mind on the tip of a needle. I am filled with gratitude at being able to experience the feeling of total connectedness to the energy of my God presence. Not only do I love the extraordinary feelings of peace, safety, and joy but I also love the fact that I have achieved the goal of being able to hold my mind on that point. I am elated.

HE APPEARS IN THE AIR

Eventually, it becomes automatic to enter that state of pure bliss. As I practice holding that state, I become aware that the presence is becoming stronger. It becomes so strong that it feels like someone is standing in the room with me.

One day, as I look at the place in my room where I feel the presence, I begin to see the image of a person. At first, the image is a blurry outline of a body. It becomes clearer and the details begin to fill in as I hold my attention on it.

I continue to focus and begin to see the image of a slender, medium-height man. He has dark brown hair that is cut into a bowl shape. He wears a shimmering, luminescent white robe with purple and golden colors in it. His eyes are brown, soft, deep, and full of compassion. They are so gentle and kind, I know I can trust him completely. His presence seems to pierce through to my soul, causing me to feel deeply loved and honored.

I know he is not a live, physical person. He looks solid, yet he is floating in the air near my bed. There is a strong feeling of familiarity about him. I feel as if I know him. I realize that he is the God presence that I have felt for so long. Now he is visible to me.

Although his body appears to be very youthful, the feeling of his expansive wisdom is perceptible. He is emanating love, kindness, and an energy that is so strong, I feel as if I were being electrified with love, a love that penetrates every cell of my being.

Nothing else in my life before this even comes close to the ecstasy of experiencing his presence so "physically." His love is so tangible that I feel totally safe. In fact, I never even think of being scared. I somehow know that I have found my spiritual teacher; he is the presence that has been with me since the baptism. He doesn't have to say anything to me to confirm our relationship. I just know who he is when I see him. I feel we have been together forever and ever for an eternity of life-times. I am excited to meet him at last. His name is Kuthumi or the master K.H.[*]

VISITING CITIES OF LIGHT

The next day, I rush home from school and run to my loft. I lie down, focus on the point, and go into that state of bliss again. When I close my eyes, I feel the presence of my teacher Kuthumi. He materializes in front of me, floating in the air and tenderly offers me his hand. I know he wants me to go with him somewhere. I reach up from my bed and place my hand in his. The moment of contact sends electrifying chills through my entire being.

"I look back at my body on the bed while floating above it..."

As our hands meet, my spirit lifts up out of my body. As it does so, I experience lightness and an incredible sense of freedom that is completely exhilarating. I look back at my body

---

[*] At the time, I didn't call him by name. For reader clarity, I use Kuthumi throughout the book. We all have a name that we are known by in the spirit realm. It was years later I learned that his name is Kuthumi or the master K.H., which was his name in his last embodiment on Earth.

on the bed while floating above it and I realize it has gone into a sort of dormant sleep state. I still feel attached to it and know instinctively that I will be aware if anything happens to it. If anybody walks into the room, my soul will immediately return.

While I am out of my body with my teacher, Earth time stands still as if it were frozen in that moment. Even though it seems as though I were gone for hours, it is mere minutes on Earth. As we move along, I become more acclimated to being in my soul body. It is pain free and so much more comfortable than my physical body. I love the feeling of freedom it gives me; I am flying through space.

In fact, the longer I stay out of my denser physical body, not only do I become more comfortable but I also become aware of who I really am and what life is all about. It feels so expansive to experience my true self. Like the genie let out of the little bottle, I feel my limitations fall away and I have access to all knowledge. I finally know the answers to all my unanswerable questions.

We are moving through space at an accelerated pace and we are moving into a different vibratory dimension. Very quickly, we approach a beautiful city of incredible light. It is breathtaking. "Where are we going?" I ask Kuthumi mentally.

He answers in a flash with a telepathic picture. "We are visiting the library."

"My favorite place! I love libraries," I exclaim excitedly.

As we approach the city of light, I am delighted to see the beauty and splendor of this magnificent place. It is brilliantly colored with large, perfectly landscaped gardens and plants of every imaginable kind. There are fountains and waterfalls everywhere. Flowers cascade from planters and vines trellis down buildings. The air is filled with the exotic fragrances of these living jewels. Much of the architecture in this city reminds me of ancient Greece or Rome.

There are marble pillars, arches, and statues carved in great detail. Painted scenes on some of the pillars remind me of different eras I have read about on Earth. The powerful looking buildings are massive and stately. Some are modern; some are more classical with Roman arches. One I see is circular, made of stone with a domed roof.

Scintillating gold and jewels are used to decorate the buildings, making them resplendent. Many jewels are as large as dinner plates. Here they use jewels as we would use glass. Giant china vases stand in some of the gardens. They have histories inscribed on them in pictures like a divine version of the hieroglyphic inscriptions found in Egypt

There is one overwhelming mighty spiritual presence in this entire place that I become instantly aware of. It is an omnipresent force that permeates the atmosphere and all here are cognizant of it and honor it. This presence is more than words can describe because it is in everything and it is everything, but, at the same time, it seems to have a consciousness of its own. It is an energy that is so peaceful, loving, and comfortable that I never want to leave its company.

This wondrous, divine energy never leaves me while I am visiting the city of light. I can always feel its awareness of me, yet it does not feel intrusive. It is totally accepting of my being and actions. My teacher is also aware of this divine energy that surrounds us, as is everyone there.

A luminous essence lights the buildings. It is never dark. Light seems to come from some limitless supply of cosmic energy. If more light is needed, this essence interprets the need and produces it as desired or dims it when needed. Electric lights, as we know them, are nowhere to be seen. There is no visible heating and cooling system either; everything just remains at a perfect comfortable temperature all at times.

Many spiritual beings congregate in the various parts of the city of light. Some of the beings are resting, some are doing projects, and others are studying or teaching. They all look like normal human beings, except that they are extremely beautiful and in perfect health. The atmosphere is what one might imagine Socrates and his pupils enjoying in ancient Greece.

THE LIBRARY

We approach a massive building with an architecture that reminds me of the Parthenon, but it is ten times the size. There are about 200 steps leading up to this building, which sits on a knoll. It is marble with a portico held up by four massive marble pillars, two on each side of the huge entry doors.

The doors are at least 20 feet high and made out of a shiny rose-colored metal that looks like brass and copper combined. The embossed designs on the doors are extremely beautiful and seem to convey a story, although I don't know what it means. These doors are much too heavy for a person to open and there are no door handles. To enter, people either go through the doors or they open automatically when people arrive. Several beings enter as I watch.

I am in awe of this magnificent building. Kuthumi tells me that this is the library. I am very excited because I love libraries and this is the biggest one I have ever seen. I telepathically ask Kuthumi if we can go inside. He answers that I will go in tomorrow because I need to return to my body now. Before I can reply, I am traveling very quickly in reverse.

The next instant, I feel myself slipping back into my body and experiencing the density of the Earth plane. I feel heavy and thick. My mind becomes slower and less knowledgeable. "I can't wait until tomorrow," I think to myself.

Later, as I go to feed my four dogs and five aquariums of fish, do my homework, and eat dinner, I think about my experiences in the city of light. It is so beautiful there and everything is in perfect order, clean, and neat. I wish my house were more like that.

BEING OUT OF BODY

All the following day, I can barely wait for school to end so I can be with my teacher and go to the city of light. I am so excited that I can hardly stand it. When I get home from school, I go straight to my loft. My next adventure is about to begin.

When I reach the point, my teacher appears immediately. I don't have to call him or invite him; he just knows when I am ready. He extends his hand to me. So I reach up and put my hand in his. The minute I touch him, my energy quickens and I experience myself being lifted up out of my body. I feel so free, so light, and so excited. The expansive knowledge and eternal wisdom instantly fills my mind. Once again, I sense we are traveling faster than the speed of light.

After a few minutes, we approach that magnificent city of light. I am awestruck by the beauty of the place. The next thing I know, we are moving toward the library itself. I don't remember how we get in; we are just there. The massive doors did not open for us. We must have gone through the walls.

When we stop, I look around. It is awe-inspiring. The inside is massive like the outside but the decor is more like a study with dark wood and heavy beams. The tables are set in rows at least thirty feet long, and huge chairs of heavy wood with large armrests line the tables. They have a cloth of ornate material on the padded cushions and seat backs. It looks like an ancient library and a place for serious study.

"This library is called the Hall of Records," Kuthumi explains. "It contains records of every soul and includes every

81

lifetime they have lived on Earth. It also contains the entire history of planet Earth." I am filled with a deep respect for all the wisdom that is contained here.

LIFE BOOKS

From floor to ceiling and wall-to-wall, I am completely surrounded by books. There are ladders that run along the bookshelves, although I never see anyone use them. The librarians can just appear in the air next to the book they want, float up to it, or just have it appear in their hand. Kuthumi and I sit down at one of the massive tables. The librarian retrieves my life book for me. I don't have to tell him what I want; he knows who I am and just brings my book. He somehow understands the intention of my visit. Perhaps it has been made known to him telepathically by my teacher.

The librarian seems to delight in being of service to us. He sets my book on the table in front of me. The book is not a normal book like we have on Earth. It is about five feet wide and three feet tall when opened. It sits on a stand like a computer monitor. It forms a screen in front of me, which is controlled by my thoughts. When I view the screen, it is as if I were in the book because I can't see the edges, only the screen. As I look into the book, it is as though I were looking at my life from the perspective of my guardian angel, watching over me.

Kuthumi communicates, "What I want you to do today is to review several excerpts from your current life to get a better understanding of why you made certain choices for this lifetime. Why you chose your mother and father, for example." He watches me get started then disappears. I feel Kuthumi leave and the next time I look up he is gone from the library. I know he will return when I finish with my lessons.

I begin my review by thinking what I want to see. It appears instantly on the screen. As I watch these movie excerpts from my current life, I can tell what all the participants are feeling and thinking as they live that part of my life with me. Of course, I can feel my own emotions and know my thoughts. Because I know what they are thinking and feeling, truth is evident. Nothing is hidden from me.

It is so engrossing, sitting here in the library, seeing the things I have just lived through that I forgot about. As I watch, I understand everything that is happening from the perspectives of everyone involved, not just my own. In addition to that, I know the life plan of every person involved in each scene. I am aware whether or not they are making progress toward the goals they have set up for their lifetime. This is true for all the things they do in each life scene.

I now understand why I have experienced certain situations in my life. They were planned before I even came to Earth. I see what lessons I am working on and why I had chosen many of the events that have already occurred in my lifetime. I see how my interactions with others helped me to deepen my understanding and compassion. I review many interactions with my family and friends the way they actually happened. I look at how I interacted with my mother, father, stepfather, brother, sisters, and others.

After a while, I become comfortable with how the life book works and understand more as the memory of having done this before returns to me. Then I get more creative. I go back and change how I react in certain situations in my life. The "book" then plays out the full scenario with those changes and shows me how my life could have gone had I made those decisions instead of the ones I did make. I continue to play with the book, trying out different ideas. I am searching for the best way to help myself and those around me achieve our goals for the lifetime I am viewing.

It is mesmerizing and fun. Time flies; so, before I know it, Kuthumi is back sitting beside me, ready to take me back home. Reluctantly, I close the huge book. The librarian comes to take it without being told, again interpreting my need before I say anything.

I have gained a much higher level of comprehension during this exercise. I now feel better about some of what I thought were unfortunate circumstances in my life. Now I understand that I planned these events to increase my growth and learning in this life. I decided these things in heaven before I was even born.

Kuthumi says it is time to go back to my body on Earth. He explains that tomorrow I will have a very special lesson that will increase my understanding of how things work on Earth. No sooner have we begun the journey than we are arriving, and I find myself falling back into my body. I experience the heaviness coming over me again. I am back home in my little loft.

As I do my chores that night, I feel more joyous and loving than usual. I am determined to treat people better because of what I learned in my lesson today. It really makes sense to me to treat other people as well as possible, especially now that I realize I am going to be reliving their experiences and feelings in my life reviews. They are not totally separate from me, as I had believed. It is like each of us is part of a larger organism that evolves collectively. It is a sobering but awesome understanding I receive from my lesson today.

CHAPTER FIVE - LESSONS FROM KUTHUMI ABOUT HEAVEN AND EARTH

EVERYTHING IS ENERGY

At school, I am antsy and very excited. I try to stay focused on my schoolwork, but my mind races ahead to the meeting with Kuthumi, which will happen soon. He said he is going to show me something special, and I am so full of anticipation, I can hardly wait another minute to find out what it is.

It is very difficult for me not to be able to share my excitement with anyone. I can't explain my visits to the city of light or mention Kuthumi to my friends or relatives because they would not understand. I love going there and am thrilled about all that I am learning. I certainly do not want to stop. It is a secret I don't even share with my sister, Teresa, who is my greatest confidant.

School finally ends, but the bus ride home seems to take forever. I pass the time by talking with my sister and playing a game with our friends. The object of the game is to toss food over the heads of everyone else to our best friends without anyone intercepting it. It is great fun. We actually bring things every day to play this game and compete for who can get the best snacks to throw. We wonder if my mother ever questions why we take so many snacks each day. Finally, when the bus arrives at my stop, I jump off and run to my house.

I can't wait to get to the city of light and my special lesson. When I get to my little loft, I look out the window. This always helps me to calm myself. I love to watch the wind blowing through the grass and trees. I close my eyes and envision the scene outside again. My mind begins to relax and I move toward the point. As I arrive, my teacher appears, emanating love that fills me completely. His love for me is so unconditional that I always feel comfortable in his presence. His hand is already reaching for mine as I arrive at the point. So I reach out for it, I feel his touch as an energy of complete safety and happiness. I am released from my body and our energies coalesce. Once again the lightness and freedom penetrate my being. We fly together at tremendous speed toward the city of light.

THE MANSION

Although I expect to go to the library, we pass over it and soon approach another building that is close by. It is a large mansion with beautiful woodwork on the exterior. Exquisite gardens with flowering trees, fountains, and green lawns surround this mansion. It all looks very solid just as things do on Earth, but it is beautiful beyond anything I've seen there. When we enter the mansion, my teacher takes me to a large room that is furnished with the most incredible furniture I have ever seen. It is a combination of antique Victorian and Asian styles. I am so taken by its grandeur that I just stand there and drink it all in for a few moments. We soon move on to another room where my lesson is to take place. This instruction room is as large as a living room in the White House. Once again the luminous background light is present. I sit down on a couch to wait for the lesson.

Kuthumi holds out his hand and instantly a glass of water appears in it, which he holds out toward me. The glass of water begins to take on a different perspective for me. I am able to see deeply into its structure as though I were looking through a powerful magnifying glass. The very particles of the glass and the water itself are visible to me. I can see how they are linked together. The glass particles are connected to the water particles and to the air particles and to everything else in the room. The entire room is a sea of energy particles vibrating at different frequencies. It is all connected; there is nothing animate or inanimate that is not part of this same whole.

Everything is vibrant and charged with light. I am also part of this sea of particles. I can see how my particles connect to the air particles, which connect to every other thing in the room. "We really are all one. Wow, this is incredible!" I exclaim. I realize that each thing has a certain individual identity, but is part of a larger picture. Each drop of water is a part of the whole ocean, yet each drop is separate in and of itself. I am fascinated by the connection between all these things.

Then my view expands outward like a camera zooming out. I see the Earth and myself in it. I can see how I am part of the world and everything in it is made up of those same energy particles. Again, at this larger level, I see all parts of life are connected to each other, yet each thing is individual at the same time.

From there, my vision turns inward, as if the camera were now zooming in. I see myself as if I were inside my body that's lying on my bed. There is a part of me that is beautiful and colorful. This contains my essence, the part that makes me who I am. I guess it would be what is referred to as my spirit. I have the sense that this part of me is an energy that is eternal and different from the other particles that form my body.

I see how my physical Earth body is dense and separate from that essence, yet integrated with it. This essence is my connection to the source of the things I see outside of me. I can see how the energy of myself emanates out from my body and affects everything and everyone I come in contact with. "I can't believe this!" I exclaim. "It never occurred to me before that I could have any effect on a plant or a chair." Of course, I knew that I affected other people with my "energy" via my moods, but I didn't know how much I affected them. And I never suspected that I had an effect on inanimate objects.

I am viewing firsthand that there is no real "solid" mass to anything. Everything is really just energy and light vibrating. It's as if it were all made of air. The whole world I live in is a projection on a living screen instead of a fixed, solid reality.

Behind everything is an empty space or dark field out of which the particles forming all matter emerge. It seems to be the source of it all. This space is how creation takes place, everything emanates from that energy. God is the energy of the empty space or void, the source of the particles that form the matter, the power behind it all.

When we finish with this lesson, Kuthumi nods to me and instantly we begin the return trip to my room where my body is lying on the little bed by the window. Whereas before, the return trip seemed to take more time, now I just seem to arrive instantly. Before I know it is happening, I feel myself getting heavy as I slip back into my physical body. It is over all too fast. I could have stayed forever exploring that new reality.

It seems to me that we were gone for several hours, but I know that, by Earth time, I have only been gone a few minutes. In that heavenly reality, it seems like a long time, but time there always feels like it has no beginning or ending, as if it were suspended in eternity, a completely different perspective of time than on Earth. It seems as though time stands still.

I lie on my bed for several hours after returning, just thinking about what I have just experienced. I realize that the bed under me is not really solid; it is made up of particles and they are moving at incredible speed. The air I am breathing is a part of me, and it is alive in a real, energetic sense. I affect it with my feelings, thoughts, and with every breath I take. As I look around my bedroom, I am fascinated, wondering what each item in my room really looks like.

I review the concepts I learned. First of all, everything in heaven and Earth is made of particles of energy. Second, everything is affected by my thoughts, feelings, and will. Third, the most important part of the particles is the empty space between them, the nothingness, for want of a better word to describe it. Fourth, this nothingness is the source from which everything here on Earth is formed and appears to us as solid and real. Fifth, this energy can be used to make something, which can be dissolved into the nothingness, and that same energy is then used to make a new thing.

All things can be formed from the nothingness between particles. In this sense, something comes from nothing, but that nothing is obviously something too.

I think about all of this in terms of religion too. When my minister says that "God is everywhere and God is in everything," I now understand what he means, because that is exactly what I saw. But even more than that, I am a part of "God" too. We are all part of it, all one, all connected via this energy. God or spirit can never "leave us" as spirit is in us, a part of our very fiber and breath. God is the power of creation, and the intelligence of it, the energy and creative force behind the nothingness, the energy soup from which everything is born.

I do see, however, that we all have an individual identity within this field of life. I am me and I am not another, even though we are one, connected in this spiritual energy. We each have our own consciousness, and do our own creating, yet what we create is affected by the group consciousness and group creation.

Kuthumi showed me in this first lesson how this energy is a continuum, one stream of energy flowing from the person, to the air, and to the physical objects in our environment. All we see is just energy, vibrating at different frequencies. The reality is that there is no separation between us, only a sense of separation created in our own perceptions. That night, I fall asleep contemplating all that I learned about this planet I live on. Things certainly are different from what they appear to be.

PAST LIFE LESSONS

The next day, I wake up, and begin to realize how my life is much different than I previously thought. I am filled with joy and awe as I look around and see life in a new way. This has been only my first lesson about Earth, but already I am

89

changed. I look forward to my day more than I ever have before. Although I am usually a happy person, recently I feel even happier. Kuthumi's presence is with me even when I am at school. He is with me everywhere I go now, although he doesn't interfere. He just observes what I am doing.

My life has become an exciting adventure. Each day I travel to the city of light with my teacher and learn lessons that are precious gems compared to the lessons I learn in elementary or Sunday school.

Today, I return to the library to learn about my past lives. We arrive at the library where Kuthumi escorts me to a long wooden table and instructs me what to review today. My book of life or life book appears as I sit down. The screen opens before me and I thought project to it what I want to see. It just comes onto the screen as if by magic.

The scenes play out and I am completely enthralled. I see that if I had made different choices in my last life, they would have led to a better outcome. I am allowed to try several different choices and see how each would have played out in that particular life. I see the consequences if I had decided to stay in Ireland and submit to an arranged marriage, if I had ended my mourning for Edward and joined his parents in their social circle, and if I had moved on with my life and found a new love.

This is a lesson on how my choice to be angry and hateful in my last life did not serve me as well as being forgiving and accepting. This struggle has repeated for several lifetimes, and I have tried to master it by cultivating understanding and compassion.

As I finish my lesson, Kuthumi arrives to take me home to Earth. He just shows up at the right time. My teacher knows when I finish my lesson without me thinking or saying anything to him. We leave the library, and, in a flash, I am back in my bedroom. As I am falling back into my body, I remember my new goal, to bring back as much knowledge from the heaven world as I can.

I just gained an incredibly expanded awareness and knowledge. I try with all my might to hold onto it. As I sink down into my physical body, I repeat to myself, "I will remember, I will remember, I WILL REMEMBER!"

However, as I make the transition into my body, much of what I have gained is lost. I still remember my lesson and meeting with Kuthumi, but the access to heaven's infinite knowledge base is gone. It slips out of my mind like quicksilver. My frustration at trying to pull this information over to this side feels overwhelming. I sit up on my bed knowing that I have just lost the answers to life's most important questions. It is painful to realize that I cannot bring all of that higher knowledge with me. It evaporates in an instant. "My brain can't contain it," I think to myself. This human brain is so limited; it just can't contain such vast information. It feels like I am trying to pour the whole ocean into a little bottle. Nevertheless, I am determined to try harder next time.

Eventually I quit thinking about not being able to bring it all back with me, and I go on with my day. I realize there is nothing I can do about that problem presently. However, it won't stop me from trying again and again if necessary. It is almost an obsession with me; I am so intent on doing it.

HOMEWORK HELP

The next day, Kuthumi takes me to the beautiful mansion and we sit down in what appears to be the living room. I now know that this room is a room Kuthumi has just created for my lesson today. He creates it mentally as a thoughtform, projects that out from himself, and it appears perfectly. Everything seems physical, but I know all of it can disappear any minute and be replaced by something that works better for today's lesson.

91

As I sit down, I telepathically tell my teacher, "My homework is so boring and difficult. I don't understand why it is important for me to learn this stuff that I'm doing in Earth school."

He smiles knowingly as if he knew my question before I asked. He answers me by showing me why it is important for me to learn, and why it is in my best interest to do well in school. To illustrate his point, he projects several scenes of my future in this life and how I will use my accumulated knowledge. This projects directly from his mind into mine. He sure gets his point across with complete accuracy, and I totally understand him. Of course, his reasoning is solid.

He also shows me, using my own past memories, how I feel better about myself when I do a good job on my school assignments. Then he illustrates how this accrued information and wisdom allows me to understand how the physical world works. This, in turn, makes it easier to live on Earth and succeed in my life mission assignments here. I am feeling very grateful for the compassion he shows me in answering my questions.

"Thank you," I project to him. As with any normal 11-year-old, I have endless questions, and Kuthumi has the patience to answer all of them.

He continues my lesson by helping me with my school homework, especially math, a subject I have never done well in. It is so easy to understand when he explains it. I learn later that one of Kuthumi's embodiments was Pythagoras, who had a profound understanding of mathematics. He encourages me to learn my Earth school lessons well and to help others by sharing my passion for learning with them.

On Monday, my school lessons seem to fly by. I can easily comprehend what the teacher is saying. I finish my work in record time, then I look around to find someone to help, as Kuthumi suggested. In our classroom, we are allowed to help others when we finish our own work. After helping a few students, I discover that I really enjoy my new role. It is good to help others and spread the love of learning. Now, I am not only hooked on learning but also sharing it with others.

That night, as I lie in my bed before going to sleep, I think of my teacher and telepathically send him a giant "thank you" not only for the help with my homework but also for the positive change his tutoring has made in my life.

Later, as I receive my grades and they are all A's, it encourages me even more. My teachers are pleased but a bit mystified by the sudden change in my attitude and abilities. Little do they know where it is coming from, and I am certainly not going to tell them. I continue to improve and become an excelling student. Previously, I had been only an average and struggling student.

UNDERSTANDING PEOPLE: THE ICEBERG ANALOGY

On Sunday after church, it is time to meet my teacher again. We fly quickly to the city of light, and then to an inner sanctuary. Celestial music plays, but its source is not apparent. Somehow I perceive it is just right for the moment. I don't have to know its source.

My teacher brings me to what appears to be a study. A beautiful crystal chandelier hangs overhead and lights the room with a pleasant glow. This chandelier has no light bulbs but glows with an ever-present illumination. The room is beautifully decorated with ornate furnishings. The wood walls and finely polished furniture are so shiny I can almost see my reflection in them. Everything is always so clean here. There is never anything dirty or dusty and it is all so orderly. I can't help wishing my house were this clean. Shelves of fine leather-bound books adorn one of the walls. I feel at home, as if this were my real home. Although I never want to leave here, I know, in my heart, I will return to my loft after my lesson today is over.

Many of my lessons center on understanding people. Today I have a burning question on my mind concerning a person in my life. Once again, Kuthumi knows the question before I ask, since he can easily read my thoughts. This has been on my mind all day. I want to know why certain people get angry so often. I am particularly interested in knowing about a man who lives in the house behind ours. He seems to be consistently mad at everyone.

Kuthumi answers, "Watch this and you will understand him in a new way." In my mind a movie begins to play by itself. This is my teacher's answer to my question. He shows me scenes from the man's past lives and his current life tests. The first thing I see is this man's evolution over his last few lifetimes, including this one. My teacher shows me how his anger began and how it progressed through these lifetimes. Kuthumi downloads this instantly and simultaneously into my mind by flashing images of major events in the man's past lives. All this happens with lightening fast speed. It takes all of a couple of seconds to cover hundreds of years. Yet, my understanding is complete, and it feels effortless.

Kuthumi shows me that this man has been making steady progress toward being less angry and more peaceful, but it is a difficult lesson for him. His development seems slow to me, and I communicate that to my teacher. He shows me several other people's lifetimes, focusing on the development of that trait. Over and over, I observe the souls striving to learn that anger is not in their best interest as a reaction to the difficulties they experience. Some people are faster and some, like this man, are slower to learn. Kuthumi explains that it is not important how fast they arrive at their soul's growth, just that they make progress. Many lifetimes are needed to gain such understanding. Wisdom comes after much life experience.

When he intuits that I have a grasp of the concept, Kuthumi expands my lesson by thought-projecting the image of a huge iceberg to me. The iceberg is more than three-quarters submerged in water. At first I do not understand, "Why are you showing me this image?" I ask. Then he explains it to me. "The part of the iceberg above the water represents the part of the man you can see when interacting with him." In other words, it represents his behavior, the angry reaction in this case.

He continues, "The part of the iceberg that is under the water represents the man's past lives and all that has happened to him in those lives. Much of this is from his most recent past lives. The pain this man has suffered in his other lives has caused much of the anger in this lifetime. He blames God and others for what happens to him. He has not yet reached the understanding that he creates much of what happens in his life for his own growth."

"This is fascinating!" I exclaim. "Now I have such a different view of this man." I sense great compassion flowing into my heart, as I think about all he has experienced. Just as I receive this understanding, Kuthumi adds a thought. "When you have compassion for all the pain this man has suffered, the bottom of the iceberg, you will have little trouble having compassion for the man's anger, the tip of the iceberg."

The iceberg is a symbol to help me remember to have compassion for people's suffering and not get so caught up in their behavior at the moment. He repeatedly reminds me that what I am observing in people's behavior is only the tip of the iceberg. There is six times more pain inside them than what I am observing on the outside. He tells me that the anger or other negative emotion is only the reflection of the pain they are experiencing inside themselves. I resolve to continue using this analogy throughout my life. It will help me to be more understanding and patient with people.

Another lesson Kuthumi teaches me is about light globes, small round lights that kill anything not wanted in my body. He tells me to activate them any time I feel something trying to invade my body. He shows me how I can make them work by telling them telepathically to attack and remove foreign things from my body. This is its defense system against disease, he explains. If anyone around me on Earth is ill, I should alert my light globes to attack and remove the offending substance. He tells me that if I have a feeling of invulnerability and ferociousness toward any disease, I can remove it from my body, using these little helpers.

My lessons continue on a daily basis. Each time my teacher comes and escorts me personally to the etheric realm. Every time, I learn more about life. We visit the library quite often. Every day is heavenly for me.

A LIFE REVIEW

On Monday, I am back at school trying my best to help others. After school, I go straight home to my bedroom and meet my teacher. Although I enjoy school now, I am enthralled with Kuthumi and my adventures in the city of light. I want to be there as much as possible. This is the highlight of my day.

Today, as we go into the library, my attention is drawn to a young man who is sitting and looking at his life book. I have the awareness that he is reviewing his present life with his guide, who sits next to him. He seems generally pleased with what he sees on the screen. He is giving himself some very good "grades" for his actions and accomplishments. We pause here to observe this man; I realize after a while that this seems to be part of my lesson today.

When the man begins reviewing how well he is doing at accomplishing the goals he set for himself, he is not as pleased. I have the feeling that he had difficulty staying focused on those goals because of the many distractions in his life. I understand how hard it is and send a ray of compassion to him. He accepts it and sends a ray of gratitude back to me.

He, like most souls, wants to accomplish as much as possible during his time on Earth. His guide listens and communicates to him that at several times in his lifetime he did make great progress, despite much opposition. The guide projects a feeling of love and support to the young man. This love lightens the man's attitude and enlivens his energy field so that it looks brighter and more vibrant. The man becomes more accepting of himself through this process. The interaction between them encourages me. I love seeing how this guide is helping the man he is working with. He is so kind and gentle, holding him only in the highest regard.

I think as I watch them, "This relaxed, accepting, and loving atmosphere encourages every person here to learn at a pace that works for them. This makes learning fun and interesting. It is certainly different from the school I am attending on Earth." As we observe the man, I see how the respect for this man's development, his needs, desires, and freedom to choose is apparent in his guide's interactions with him. It is so refreshing to see this after what I experience on Earth.

The only grades this man is receiving are the ones he gives himself. He is hard on himself, as many souls are, but he is accomplishing much toward achieving his overall long-term goals. Souls like this strive for high ideals. He is encouraged to work hard, but it is not required. I note that there is no sense of being criticized or judged. It is a totally loving experience for him in all ways.

The only consequences I observe here for "poor performance" in our Earth lifetimes is not moving on to the next higher level of evolution. It seems there are those who move quickly through the levels and waste little time on frivolous activities, but others would rather play than work most of the time. The majority of people do move forward, though, often because they become bored with the level they are at and want to experience a larger, more expansive, and challenging level. Moving forward is a very naturally flowing occurrence for most, as it is for this man. My teacher turns to me and says, "Please understand that all learning here is for the highest good and spiritual development of each soul, just as it is on Earth."

As we observe a few other souls doing similar activities, I notice that there are a few souls that get stuck on a certain level and just want to vegetate. Then their guide works with them to encourage them to move forward for their highest good. Occasionally, this requires a bit of persuasion. Of course, there are the rare souls who just do not want to do what is best for themselves and the others in their group. They are returned to Earth over and over again to repeat their lessons. These are a very small minority, however.

Kuthumi explains, "All souls do a life review at the end of each lifetime, and oftentimes, at key points during their current life too. This allows them to assess their progress and set up circumstances for greater progress toward individual life goals. Guides help souls set everything up between lives, along with their family and soul group members. The older, more advanced souls do much of this on their own. They know exactly what they did or did not do and what they need to accomplish their goals. They work out a life plan, get feedback from their guides, and include other members of their group, but much of their work is done on their own. They become masters at this process."

He continues, "Heaven is not unlike universities on Earth. We have independent study contracts like many Earth schools. It is quite similar to working on a masters or a doctorate degree. The further the student advances, the more freedom he is given to set things up for himself. The more advanced students get more advanced teachers. The advanced teachers spend less time teaching, as it is not necessary to teach advanced students as much as the younger students. Advanced students are more self-motivated and self-correcting."

HEAVENLY SCHOOLS

He reminds me that it is not exactly the same when he says, "Sometimes heaven seems much like an Earthly school system, although only in its basic structure. Although there is hierarchy, there is no subservient principle in heaven. Everyone is considered as valuable as everyone else.

"Lessons in the heaven world are much easier than those on Earth for many reasons. First of all, teachers are experts in their field and passionate about their subjects. Second, students are not in a body, so they have an unencumbered mind, which makes learning effortless and fun. Last, but not least, you can't get things wrong or get bad grades from any teacher because the object is to help the student to understand. If someone doesn't understand something, it is explained in different ways until it is made clear."

"This is such a fair system. I can't help wishing that it were the same at my school on Earth," I say out loud.

This concludes my lesson, and before I know it, I'm back in my room falling into my body in the loft. I have a lot to think about, as usual, so I lie still for a while, contemplating and trying to integrate all I have seen into my human brain. Once again I am frustrated with how difficult it is to retain the entire knowledge. Much detail is lost in the translation, but I still remember the lesson well.

FINDING MY MISSION GROUP

The next day, when I lie down and quickly focus on the "point," Kuthumi is there. So I reach out to him and he whisks me away for my lesson. I have become so accustomed to this mode of travel by now, I think, "I wonder if I can I go by myself?" He smiles at me, and states, "I do not think you are ready for that yet; always be sure to wait for me to escort you." I am happy to agree to that because I figure he knows more than I do about this kind of travel. "Perhaps when I'm older," I think, "I will be able to do this myself."

On the way to our meeting place, we pass a group of younger souls meeting in the gazebo. I send them love as I pass by. Some of them return it. I know they are younger souls because of the lessons they are studying and the support level of teachers and guides in the classroom as well as the color and intensity of the light field around them. Younger souls always receive a lot of support and structure. They do not have the powerful, brighter auras of the master teachers like Kuthumi. They need more help making decisions about their lives and understanding the lessons they encounter on Earth.

Today is a special day for me, as I am going to meet some other souls who Kuthumi calls my mission group. I understand this is a group of souls I work with to achieve certain goals on Earth. This is my first encounter with them since I left for Earth, although I have worked with them in other lifetimes. Even though we are all children at this time on Earth, we are preparing for our future mission in this lifetime by meeting in heaven to reinforce each other on Earth. We exist in both realities at one time, both heaven and Earth. Our souls are aware of these meetings, but our Earth bodies and minds are not. Although we may receive flashes of our experiences in dreams and such, we do not have the knowledge or awareness to understand it yet.

When I reach my doctors' mission group, we get together and decide to create a meadow for our meeting today. The meeting place is a group decision, which we create with our minds. Basically, we just decide to meet in a meadow, and we mentally go there.

Kuthumi takes his leave, since we are older souls and can do much work on our own. Souls in my group often choose leadership roles, since we are such an independent bunch. Quite often, we write our life goals, get approval from our guides, who make useful suggestions, and then we implement them on Earth. In our group, just as everywhere else in the heaven world, there is no criticism, judgment, or condemnation from anyone. We work together in great harmony and respect

100

for one another. I bathe in the feeling of unconditional acceptance and love from everyone I encounter here.

We begin the discussion today about our favorite topic: healing, specifically, how we can be part of a movement on Earth to promote advanced alternative healing methods. We review several options and discuss what each of us can do to make it happen on Earth. We plan at length how we can meet each other at key times in our lives to reinforce our individual and collective goals.

After talking about healing with energy and herbals and how we can use our minds as healing modalities, we move on to implementation of our goals. Our primary goal is to bring healing techniques, similar to what we now use in the heaven world, to Earth. It is so compelling that we are overjoyed at the ideas generated today. We marvel at the positive changes this will mean for people during our current lifetime.

We all get very excited and can't wait to get started on our group mission. My time is up too soon and I have to return to Earth. Kuthumi appears right on schedule. I am a bit sad to be leaving my friends because it is so much fun to meet with souls who are of like mind. But I soon find myself feeling the pull of Earth. My body becomes heavy as I slip into it once again.

MEMORY IS BLOCKED

When I return to my loft, I lie on my bed thinking about the friends in my doctors' mission group and our plans to meet each other on Earth. We have a great plan. I just hope everyone will stay on course and not forget what they are supposed to do. It makes me so happy to be able to reconnect with my group and to visit a world of complete beauty and light. Some of what I did today in the heaven world was blocked from my Earthly memory. I am aware that it has happened, but I cannot stop it. These memory blocks are imposed on me by my teacher so that I will not miss opportunities for growth by knowing too much. I know this is for my highest good, so I readily accept it as a necessity.

MOVING UP LEVELS: THE MERIT SYSTEM

Over the next few months, I rush home every day after school, go to my bedroom, and resume my travels and lessons with Kuthumi in the etheric realm. I cannot remember all the places we visit and many of the lessons he teaches me, but some of them stick. One of the best ones is what I learn about the merit system.

As we arrive at the library in the city of light, Kuthumi gives me a stack of "books" to study. "We are going to look at your family's records in this lifetime," he explains. We begin with mine. Kuthumi points out to me what things I have done that earned merit for me in the heaven world. I am surprised that it does not exactly match our value system on Earth. He says, "On Earth, you place a lot of value on obtaining material things, such as earning money and owning property. In this world, those things are important, but mostly when they are used to further spiritual goals or help others."

Kuthumi shows me one thing that I do in this lifetime that earns merit for me, that is, defending my sister. My sister Teresa was born with a cleft palate, which gave her a lisp. The kids at school often tease her mercilessly. They will sometimes physically attack her after school lets out. I am her defender and protector. I fight many battles to keep her from harm.

"Because you are brave and stand up for her against these bullies, you gain much spiritual merit," he says.

"However, when I tease my sister, I do not get any merit," I think. He looks at me with a compassionate and loving expression on his face. It makes me feel proud and a bit embarrassed at the same time. I know I shouldn't tease my sister, but it is so much fun to watch her "blow up." I resolve to do better.

I want to be like Kuthumi, so kind and caring about others. He inspires me to improve by believing in my goodness. I don't say much, but I think deeply about everything he tells me.

"On Earth, doing what you are told and fitting in is highly valued," he continues. "But, in truth, being brave enough to do what you know is ethically correct, regardless of what you have been told, is more important. Standing up for what you know in your own heart is right, just as you do when you protect your sister. This is a characteristic you have much mastery in already."

He looks at me directly with his deep brown eyes as he says, "Helping others, especially when it is difficult for you to do so, earns the most merit of all."

I understand him completely and I state in return, "You mean people are measured by how they treat others and how many people they help, not by how many things they have."

"Exactly," Kuthumi replies. "Keep this in mind when deciding what to do in each situation of your life." He emphasizes, "It is fine to have money and things, but spiritual advancement is not about that. Learning the lessons concerning the manifestation of money and earning a livelihood are among the important lessons to be mastered on Earth, but not necessarily the most important ones. You also need to learn how to take care of yourself, balance this with helping others, and many, many other lessons to become a deeper person and a master of Earth."

LITTLE THINGS MATTER

To illustrate his point, Kuthumi shows me the life books of my step-dad and his family, the Millers. This family makes a fair amount of money through their family businesses. They own several phone companies, a lumberyard, and a general store. They help many people through these avenues. I see how much they care about the people they serve and how they help them in many ways. They help the people who work in their companies as well as the people in the communities where their offices are located. Their true feelings, thoughts, and motivations are easy to see in their life books. Nothing is hidden about a person when we view them in these books.

Kuthumi states, "Because they eagerly help others, and their motives are pure and loving, the Millers gain much merit. Merit here in heaven is also given for doing things that help you gain more understanding and grow in compassion. Their experiences with their businesses allow them to grow in understanding, progress in their spiritual development, and give them many opportunities to help others. They are setting a good example for you of a balanced life, including service and financial responsibility."

As Kuthumi says this, I feel much gratitude for their being in my life. Kuthumi announces, "We must return now. Tomorrow we will look at your spiritual progress through many lifetimes."

I am excited to learn about how I have progressed in my spiritual growth and what I have done that has gained merit for me. It appears, after what I have seen today, that it is a bit different than what I had previously thought. With a sense of awe, I return to my body in the loft and settle back into my Earthly life.

MY PROGRESS REPORT

The next day passes slowly, but finally I find myself looking into the eyes of my teacher and reaching out for his hand. We soon arrive at the city of light, where we go to the library. There we sit down at a table to prepare for my lesson.

Kuthumi requests my book of life. The librarian becomes aware of our need, manifests it in his hand and quickly delivers it to us. We review my present life and many scenes

104

from my past lives. Kuthumi shows me that I have done well in many lifetimes, but in others, I have made little progress. In some lifetimes, I have really "blown it." It is an enlightening experience to see how each of my lives assists my overall spiritual growth. I have no idea how many times I have lived, but it seems like there are hundreds.

We don't speak much during this time, as it seems unnecessary. The scenes that are passing before me convey the meaning. It's like watching a movie at incredible speed and with great clarity, yet being an actor in the movie at the same time. When the scenes end, my teacher speaks again.

"You have progressed well through your lifetimes and you have gained an expanded understanding. Now you are very close to graduation to the next level of spiritual development. At each level you have been through, you have gained specific understanding and wisdom. You are about to become a teacher. You just need to deepen your compassion and forgiveness and learn that anger does not serve you as the best reaction to situations you encounter, especially that of losing those you love. As you observed in your life book, this has been a difficult test for you over many lifetimes.

"That is why you set up your life the way you did, so you could gain mastery and understanding about these things. I am here to assist you at all times. Just call upon me," he concludes.

I send a feeling of deep gratitude to my teacher for his love and caring. He receives it and returns it to me with the added understanding that my growth and advancement is linked to his own. When I progress, so does he; we are advancing together. He sends a feeling of thankfulness to me for being the person I am and doing my best. I am happy to know I am doing something for him since he has already done so much for me.

Although Kuthumi is a master teacher and quite a bit more masterful than I am, he is never condescending. He is a truly humble person. I always feel complete love and acceptance in his presence. In fact, it is hard to go back to my Earthly life because being in his presence and that loving place is so wonderful. I just want to stay with him forever. "Do I really have to go back?" I ask him. "People on Earth can be so mean, and it is so hard there. Can't I stay here with you and the others?" However, he gently reminds me that I have much work left to do on Earth. I know he is right, so I resignedly return to my Earthly existence.

I AM BRINGING IT BACK WITH ME

When I reenter my body, I have a lot on my mind. I feel a renewed dedication to do whatever is necessary to graduate to the next level by the end of this lifetime. Then I can be a teacher, like Kuthumi.

Once again, I try with all my might to bring back the knowledge from the experiences I have just had in that world. I hold on to it as long as I can, but, as usual, most of it is lost in the process of trying to transfer it into my human brain.

Although I attempt to do this every day I meet with my teacher, I think that very little of that incredible body of heavenly knowledge is permanently retained.

My lessons with Kuthumi have built a fierce determination in me to do well, and soon I am at the top of my class. I also begin to spend my spare time at school helping other kids who are struggling. I try to follow Kuthumi's example and treat all people with the same compassion he shows me. But it isn't easy. People can be very cruel, especially kids. I often long for the heaven world where everything is so perfect and everyone so loving and kind.

106

WE ARE ALL CREATORS: MY HORSE MANIFESTATION

I often become frustrated with how long it takes to do things on Earth. When I am with my teacher in his world, he manifests everything he needs right when he needs it for my lessons. It is effortless. He just makes it appear. I want to do it too. He explains to me that I can't do it as fast because on Earth, manifestation is slowed down. That way, we don't hurt one another on a bad day if we are angry or out of control. But there was one thing I really wanted to manifest in my life. More than anything, I wanted a horse of my own.

When I was six years old, I decided I had to have that horse. I wanted one so much, that I literally bugged my mother daily. She had many reasons why we couldn't have a horse. They didn't even faze me. I would not give up and was determined to overcome her objections. For instance, she claimed we didn't have a place for a horse to live. So I tried to build a fence out of boards and rope around our spare lot so it would have one.

I was obsessed with this goal and would do anything to be around horses and ponies. One day, I walked four miles outside of town to see a friend's pony. My mother was frantic because I had not told her where I was going, and was missing for hours. She called the police to look for me. We lived in a very small town. When I arrived at my friend's house, her mother called my mom, who promptly picked me up and took me home, much to my dismay. I was very disappointed that I did not get to visit the pony after that long walk. It didn't seem so far when we drove there in the car. I simply thought I could just walk over and see it without telling my mother because I wouldn't be gone long. So much for that idea.

This desire to have a horse was so strong, that I even imagined what it would be like to have the horse in our garage. I pretended it was there at times just to feel what it would be like to have my horse. Yet even now, at 11-years old, my horse had yet to appear.

So when I see Kuthumi that afternoon, I know what I want to ask him. As he comes to my loft that day, he seems to anticipate my question, as always. I soon find out, we are going to a different place. For my lesson today, he creates the most beautiful white-sand beach I have ever seen. It is picture perfect. As we sit down on the powdery white sand, he begins to explain to me why some people don't get what they desire.

He shows me that sometimes they block themselves by not keeping focused on their goals. At other times, they are not willing to do the work necessary to attain it. Then at times, it is not in the highest good for them or those around them. It can also be a timing issue. Their desire can even be in conflict with their life goals.

Kuthumi tells me that no energy is wasted. All of our interactions are meaningful. It is an intricate and delicately interwoven dance we do down here. Our growth and understanding is all integrated with our friends' and family members' growth and understanding. We all grow together. He shows me that we do have the power to alter our life with our thoughts, feelings, and actions. This power, however, is always in a balance with our life goals. He illustrates this with a video downloaded straight into my head. I see how I have written a script for my life before my birth, and how that script fits in with the collective or group goals of the people that are around me. He points out that I can't always get everything I desire because it may not be for my highest good or growth, it may not fit in with the group goals I had agreed to work on, or the timing may be off. Persistence I do not need, since I have plenty of that already.

"Matter," he explains, "is quickly and easily changed from one form to another. On the Earth, however, matter changes slowly, but it is still subject to the powers of creation you exert upon it. It is just much slower and requires much more effort or desire to manifest something there."

As I sit on that magnificent beach, listening to Kuthumi, I am convinced that he is right. I can see how easy it is for him to create anything he desires. I long for the day when I will be like him. At least now I understand why my every desire does not come true on Earth. However, I am not ready to give up on manifesting my horse at all.

The more time I spend in the heaven world, the more I come to the conclusion that the world I live in on Earth is an illusion, that life here is not as I observe it to be. I realize that, in my limited human brain, I do not have the ability to know things as they truly are. It can't contain the whole truth. The rules I think I know are not the ultimate rules; they are just the rules for the time I am on Earth. It will always be difficult to understand the way things really work while I am in my body.

Kuthumi and I sit in silence as I ponder these things and drink in the vision of beauty all around me. This new awareness alters my view of the world. When I look back at my teacher, his eyes are smiling at me. The lesson is over; instantly we are back on Earth.

In my loft, I review the lessons of the day, trying to retain as much of it as I can, but knowing that much will be lost. I can't help but feel the frustration again. If only I could remember it all.

THE MYSTERY LADY

Each day, I become more excited about my life. School is becoming much more fun because I am doing so well. Kuthumi has helped me find my passion for learning and instilled in me the desire to excel. I want more than ever to be like him. Although I am thoroughly enjoying my lessons at school, they can't compare with what I am learning in the heaven world. I am particularly intrigued about my lessons today because Kuthumi has mentioned we will have a guest.

As usual, Kuthumi arrives on schedule to meet me for my lesson after school. I am whisked away to the city of light. It fills me with joy and a feeling of lightness that is true ecstasy. Today we are going to the mansion again to continue my lesson on how to create using the mind. I am looking forward to understanding more about this.

When we settle down to study, I notice the guest is already present. The most stunningly beautiful lady I have ever seen is sitting across the room to the left side of us. She has long dark hair that is slightly wavy. Her eyes are brown, extraordinarily soft, and filled with love. They appear to be deep endless pools, the kind of eyes that draw people in, eyes so profound and infinite that one can gaze into them and lose all sense of time and space. She has flawless olive-colored skin and wears a multicolored silk gown wrapped around her body like a sari. It is made of the most unusual colors I have ever seen: a mixture of gold, coral, and tan that is so shiny, it almost glows. This gown contrasts with her dark skin, giving her a look of royal elegance.

Her presence is so peaceful that it permeates the room like a mysterious mist, and we are enveloped in it. I just want to bathe in her presence forever. Never in my life have I seen such beauty and peace; she is the picture of perfection. I am so impressed by her that I can hardly take my attention off her long enough to do my lesson. Truthfully, I can't remember what my lesson was that day. I am so entranced by her eyes and her presence that I do not recall anything else that happens.

I notice that my teacher is aware of her, but he does not tell me who she is or why she is here. He only says that she is here to observe my lesson. I know I cannot speak to her so I don't try to communicate with her. But her spirit is so powerful that I can't ever forget her. She is probably communicating with my teacher without me "hearing" her, since many of the master teachers do that here. The fact that I cannot hear them communicate leads me to believe that she is either a student of Kuthumi or she is his teacher.

The way beings in this heavenly world "talk" to each other without disturbing or sharing what they have to say with others around is simple. They simply change their intention to broadcast only to certain individuals and not to the others, much like a ham radio can tune into different frequencies.

When my lesson is over, Kuthumi indicates that it is time to go. This time I really don't want to go back. I want to stay with him and find out more about this mysterious lady. He senses my resistance and understands my curiosity. "When the time is right," he says, "you will find out all about her. If you wish, she can be present at your next lesson." I am sure my face lit up to show my pleasure at such an invitation.

My teacher sends a telepathic confirmation back to me that I will see the mystery lady again next time. My heart leaps to think that she will come to my lesson again. I am so happy and deeply honored. Now I have something even more wonderful to look forward to. I return to my Earthly existence with a happy heart. Although I have only seen her once and never spoken to her, she seems familiar to me and I immediately feel close to this lady. It is like I knew her before I met her. It must be from sometime in a past life that I can't recall.

I beam love and gratitude to my teacher, and we move out of the mansion back to my waiting body. This time, as I reenter my body, I know that I will not forget that mystery lady. She is unforgettable.

As is my usual procedure I lie on my bed, envisioning the meeting with her, wondering who she is, why she is attending my lessons, and wishing that tomorrow would come soon. The next thing I know, it's dinnertime, and I head downstairs.

WE ALL KNOW THE TRUTH

Saturday arrives and I have chores to do. I finish them quickly, and then play with my sister for a while. My mom works another job on Saturdays, leaving us with the nanny, so I have some time to myself. As soon as I can, I go to my loft.

My teacher appears as usual and we move, hand in hand, toward the city of light. We arrive at the mansion and sit down to begin my lesson. No sooner have we begun than the mystery lady appears and I find myself entranced once again with her profound presence and radiant beauty. Her eyes sparkle with light and energy. We do not speak, just as before. I know she is there just to observe and not to teach me. Today, I am determined to pay closer attention to my teacher. I force myself to focus on his lesson and not be so distracted by this intriguing visitor.

Today Kuthumi shows me how everyone can really tell the difference between the truth and lies. "You cannot really deceive others," he says. "Everyone knows the truth or a lie by its vibration, so when you lie, you are only fooling yourself. It is a form of self-deception." I think about how I lie to my mother and nanny sometimes to protect myself from an unjust punishment. In my household, it seems that lying is a form of self-defense, and I have become quite adept at it. However, Kuthumi never mentions that. In fact, he never criticizes or reprimands me for anything that I am doing in my life on Earth. He understands that I am doing the best I can to manage my life situations.

"The truth has a certain vibration or ring to it and so does a lie," he continues. "You only think people don't know the difference and that you 'get away with it.' You don't get away with anything."

He shows me how everything I say is recorded in infinite detail in my book of life for me to review between lives. Since I have already studied this, I know what he says is true.

112

Witnessing in my book how I have been hurt by lies other people told about me and how I have hurt others by lying is very enlightening.

I know that I also use my life book to decide what situations to set up for myself in my next lives. This is an aid to my spiritual growth. For example, if I need to learn the value of truthfulness, I can set up situations in my next life to help me gain a greater understanding of why it is in my best interest to be truthful. Even though it is painful at times, this helps me become a more honest, compassionate, and loving person. My understanding of truth is expanded and deepened.

I realize, at that moment, that I have done this in my present life. I put myself in a family situation where it is tempting to lie to avoid punishment. And I am lying under certain circumstances to protect myself. I resolve to work on this aspect of myself by trying to find ways to tell the truth even if it hurts. Kuthumi continues, "Speaking the truth can help you to graduate from this level. When you speak the truth, it gives you more power."

When he says that telling the truth will help me graduate, he has my full attention. My burning desire is to move on to the next level of my spiritual growth, to become more like the master teachers. I have met many of them, since they occasionally come to teach me and interact with me as I visit various places in the heaven world with my teacher. They are like the parents every child would love to have. Since I am a child, I look up to them and want to grow up to be just like them.

Before we leave, I glance at the mystery lady, I would love to be as beautiful as she is. In body, mind, and spirit, she is the vision of purity. I am so loved in her presence and the presence of my teacher. I experience overwhelming joy.

Then I look back at Kuthumi. I know my lesson is over and it is time to go. Although I can't bear the thought of leaving them, I know I must, so off we go. I love my visits to the heaven world and I look forward to tomorrow when I can visit again. Unfortunately for me, it is not destined to last much longer.

Once again, I lie in my loft and bask in the afterglow of their love. I have never known such love in my entire life; it fills my heart to overflowing.

Shah Jahan [Kuthumi] and Mumtaz Mahal by Joyce Johnson

I think about the lady again. She is still a mystery to me, because she is the only one in that realm who does not communicate with me. She is always an observer. She never interacts with me, just watches my lessons. I wonder how she is related to my teacher. Is she a partner, or student, or, perhaps, even his teacher? I wonder if I will ever know.

As always, the needs of my life draw my attention to the present moment. My responsibilities are waiting for me. So I resume my life as a young girl, and go down to eat my dinner.

FUTURE LIFE PREDICTIONS

The following Monday after school, I return home to do my meditation practice and out-of-body traveling, which I have been doing for about a year now. Today, I am given a preview of my life book in the library that contains the future of my present life. Kuthumi decides which clips I should view, and they appear on the screen. This time, he controls the book and I just watch.

Kuthumi shows me myself as an adult, speaking to large audiences on some kind of speaking tour. He does not allow me to see what subject I am speaking about. That information is blocked to prevent me from gaining information before it is in my best interest to know it. I understand that it is for my highest good and I am fine with that, but do wonder who the people are that I see in my future and what I will be talking to them about.

It goes well and I enjoy my lessons with Kuthumi as usual. Upon returning to my body, I stay for a long time, considering what he showed me today. I think about the fact that part of my future is written and decided on, yet it is still somewhat up to me to fulfill my destiny. Others are depending on me to do my part to help them accomplish their life goals. Then there is my part in helping the people of our planet as a whole by my contributions and self-development. It is all so complex, yet, in heaven, it seems so simple and obvious. I marvel at the intricacy of the process. Everything is so interwoven. I think our guides must work overtime to help us do what we do down here.

CHAPTER SIX - MY MOTHER FINDS OUT

IT'S BETTER IN HEAVEN: TRYING TO EXPLAIN

About a year after I begin meeting with Kuthumi, we move to a new house in Eugene, Oregon. Finally, I have my own bedroom, but I do miss my old loft, the creek, and the trees outside my window. Now I only have a narrow yard and a city street to see when I look out. That does not stop me from doing my meditations or meeting with my teacher, though. I continue every single day after school and on weekends.

Today, as I arrive, there is a special party in the city of light. Many of the master teachers are in attendance. I eagerly watch the proceedings and enjoy the beautiful waltzes in the great ballroom. It is breathtakingly splendid. Just sitting there looking around is enough for me. The music is divine and the teachers are wearing the most incredible clothing. The colors are vibrant and jeweled tones dominate their fashion. I am honored to be included in their festivities. I don't do much but watch and talk to those who come my way, but I have a great time. It seems to me that everyone comes by, at some point, to wish me well. I do not suspect that anything is unusual.

When it is time for me to leave, I say goodbye to many of the attendees, then off to home I go. When I reach my room, time slows down for a few minutes, and, as Kuthumi gently puts me back into my body, I feel as though I were falling through space in slow motion. As I move ever so gently backward into my body, Kuthumi repeats over and over to me, "Love your mother, love your sister, love your mother, and love your sister…" I wonder why he is giving me that message, since it does not relate to anything we have just done or talked about.

He must know what is going to happen next, since he can see into the future. I sense it has some deeper meaning, and boy, am I right!   As I open my eyes, my mother enters the room. She looks at me with an expression on her face that is a mixture of curiosity and pure panic. I am very confused by her presence and the look on her face. She is not usually home at this time of day.

"What were you doing?" She asks.

I reply truthfully, "I was meeting with my teacher in the city of light, and we were at a party in a huge ballroom full of wonderful people."

At this point, she goes into a complete panic. She is sure I have been hallucinating or gone insane. My mother warns, "You must never go there again or talk to those people. They're bad for you and you could get hurt."

"But mom," I argue, "they're not evil, they're completely loving and beautiful, like angels. They aren't like people. They never say bad things or hurt anyone."

She insists, "It is not good for you to do this, and you must promise me you'll never see them again. My father talked to things that weren't there, and he had to take medicine for it. I don't want you to do it anymore. Do you understand?"

"But they're not like that; they're good to me and they help me with things. It's different," I return.

"You promise me right now that you'll never talk to them again," she demands of me.

"OK, I promise," I state reluctantly, just to satisfy her and calm her down.

"Good!" she says. "That's better, but I'm going to make an appointment with the doctor for you just in case. You must not do this kind of thing; it's what crazy people do, and they take them away to mental hospitals and put them in straightjackets. You don't want that to happen to you, do you?"

"No, I don't," I say, startled that she would think of letting someone do something like that to me, and that she might take part in making it happen.

I tell her about my teacher, Kuthumi, and the wonderful lessons I learn in the heaven world. I try my best to tell her how wonderful the teachers are, how they have absolute love, which is unconditional, unlike humans, that they're so beautiful and kind. "How could they possibly be bad?" I repeat over and over.

She is consumed by her fear, however, and absolutely insists that I stop seeing my teacher and visiting the other world. Finally, I give in and agree to her demands. I promise her that I will never go there again and speak to those beings.

She eventually leaves the room. I sit on my bed, stunned by what just happened to me. My whole wonderful world just collapsed in the matter of a few minutes. I understand her concern, but I certainly don't agree with her. I don't even cry; I am too shocked to do anything but just sit there for hours until I finally fall asleep with a heavy heart.

A VISIT TO THE SHRINK

Mom immediately takes me in for a complete psychological evaluation, which I pass with flying colors. I remember hearing the psychologist tell her that I am completely, if not somewhat above, normal, but I have an active imagination and near-genius intelligence. He assures her there is nothing at all wrong with me. He thinks my experiences are just in my imagination, like daydreaming, which many children my age do. However, he does not offer any explanation for my increased grades in school or my unusual understanding of human psychology. My teachers at school notice the grades, and, later, the understanding of psychology. They comment to my mother. No one knows why these things have happened, but I know.

Mom is better after the trip to the doctor, but still insists that I never see my teacher or go to the other world again. She will not change her mind. I very, very reluctantly agree to her demands. This is difficult for me, as I feel left alone to fend for myself in the world. Although I can still hear my teacher talk to me in my heart, by which I am somewhat comforted, it's like talking to someone on a phone with a bad connection instead of seeing him in person. It is not as effective or as much fun. My out-of-body lessons are no longer possible and I really miss those experiences.

NO MORE TEACHER

Since my teacher is no longer appearing to me on a daily basis and giving me lessons on life, I turn my attention to applying the things he taught me. He is still around if I really need his help, but I keep my word to my mother, and discontinue my meetings with him.

I really try to keep my requests to a minimum and learn to be more self-sufficient. Many times, I have the sense that he is close by, guiding and protecting me.

Some of what I learned in the cities of light Kuthumi has blocked from my memory. He did this for reasons having to do with my personal growth in this lifetime. If I were allowed to remember all that I have been shown, then my Earthly life would be too easy. It would not be enough of a challenge, or much fun either. The unexpected things keep life interesting.

MY HORSE APPEARS

My mother accepts a new job in the small town of Astoria, Oregon. We move to the top of a mountain several miles outside of town. It's a huge property with 156 fenced acres of land, a barn and a corral. There are no horses, and my mother still insists that she will not buy me one. I am undaunted in my quest, and continue to feel what it would be like to have one. I can see it in my imagination every day. I won't give up on my dream.

After nearly seven long years, the dream I had when I was six finally manifests. We are in our new house only a few weeks, when a man knocks on the door and asks my mother if I would like to have his two horses. He says that since we have all the pasture, it won't cost her anything. He will still pay for everything else they need because they belong to his daughter, so he can't sell them. His daughter is away at college, and he wants to have someone spend time with them and ride them. My mother is so shocked, she doesn't know what to say to this generous offer, so she has to accept it.

It doesn't end there. A few weeks later, another man knocks on the door, says he has three ponies, and wonders if I might enjoy having them too. I am delighted to increase my little herd, and all for free. My mother has no objections left, and I have my horses at last.

I am happy to have my desire fulfilled, and spend all my free time with my horses. Every day, when I return from school, I go straight to the barn or field to see them. Candy, the snow-white mare is my favorite. We walk together by the pond and in the woods, the orchard, the field, and the grassy hills around my house. We walk for hours until I have to go in because it's getting dark. This routine replaces my meditations with my teacher, and is a fun relaxing activity I now have to look forward to each day.

Several months later, it is all taken away from me, though, because my mother quits her job. She decides to go back to school, so we have to move, and all my dear horse friends have to go back to their owners. I am so disappointed. Horses are just not in my long-term plan this time, I guess.

We move to Portland, Oregon into a house in Ladd's Addition. I am very disappointed to be leaving my horses and my cats, rats, guinea pigs, and dogs. I had accumulated five of each on my little animal farm. For over a month, I cry myself to sleep each night. My grandma, who is staying with us for a while to help with the moving and settling process, brings me a music box. She has me listen to it as I am going to sleep. This gives me something else to focus on, so I quit crying and begin to focus on my new life in my new school.

My grandma returns to her home shortly after and my mother begins her new job and full-time studies at Portland State University. I begin my new role as primary caretaker for my three younger siblings.

JENNIFER

I am in seventh grade. During this year, a few things happen that increase my awareness of how different my life is compared to other kids.

One particular morning, the teacher asks us all to turn in our homework. I pass mine to the front, as does everyone else, except for one girl, Jennifer, the girl sitting at the desk to the right of me. The teacher, Mrs. Phillips, notices that she doesn't turn in her work and approaches her desk. "Jennifer, where is your homework?" She inquires.

"I didn't have time to do it," Jennifer replies.

"Well, that's a fine excuse. Just what were you so busy doing that you didn't have time to do your homework?" The teacher asks with a sarcastic tone. She obviously thinks Jennifer is just being irresponsible. After a long silence, Jennifer answers very quietly. The whole class is now riveted on the conversation, and I can feel Jennifer's embarrassment at being noticed in this way.

"I had to take care of my sisters, feed them dinner, clean up after them, give them a bath, and put them to bed. When I finished, it was past my bedtime, and I knew I would get in trouble from my mom if I stayed up too late."

"Well, I have never heard such poppycock," the teacher retorts. Jennifer looks shocked as Mrs. Phillips continues angrily, "No child has those responsibilities. How dare you lie to your teacher! You have an F on those assignments, and don't you ever try to lie to me like that again or I'll send you to the principal's office."

Jennifer mumbles a quivering "Yes, ma'am." In response to her distress, warm salty tears begin streaming down her cheeks. I am shocked by the teacher's lack of understanding and insensitive way of speaking to Jennifer.

"Yes, we do have responsibilities," I think to myself, feeling a deep sense of empathy for Jennifer. "I do the same thing at my home."

My heart is moved with compassion for her. I decide then and there that I will help Jennifer. What just happened to Jennifer is a shock, but what is even more enlightening to me is the teacher's statement about all that not being normal. All afternoon, I think about it. It certainly is the norm at my home. It begins to sink in for the first time that my home is different from that of other children. It seems so unfair what the teacher said to Jennifer. I can never forget the crushed look on her face.

When the school bell rings at the end of the day, I quickly find my sister and make arrangements for her to take care of things at home for me, then I catch up to Jennifer. "I know you were telling the truth to the teacher today," I say to her as we begin walking.

"How do you know?" she asks shyly.

"Because it's that way at my house. I know you do all those things because I do them too." We continue to walk and eventually reach her house. She lives closer to the school than I do, but on my path to home. "Can I come in?" I ask.

"OK, just for a minute I guess." She senses the warmth of my caring and opens up to me. She tells me all about her life, and I just listen. I know what it is like to try so hard to do everything right and only be noticed for what you don't do. It happens to me frequently at my home.

Then I suggest we get to work. "I'll help you for awhile, then I have to get home. Here, let's start with the kitchen. Boy, kids can sure mess up a house quick, can't they?" I comment.

"They sure can, and, just after you clean it up, they do it again." she replies.

"I have to go now, and get my own work done," I say after three hours have passed. Walking home, I know this visit means I will have to stay up late to get everything done at my house. Fortunately, after I explain the situation, Teresa helps me. When I finally crawl into bed, it's way past my bedtime. I think about Jennifer and wonder how it is going at her house.

The next day in class, when the teacher asks for our homework, Jennifer and I exchange glances before passing in the papers. Her homework is all done. As she passes it in to the teacher, I am grateful we got together yesterday. Having each other to understand, makes our lives much more bearable for both of us.

For many days following that one, I help her clean her house and do her homework. I give her ideas about how to get everything done quickly. It requires a lot of organization, but she finally gets it all done regularly.

We both learn to play while we work. Singing helps me to pass the time and make it more fun. I memorize many Broadway musicals this way.

Just knowing that we are here for each other, and that we have a secret, which the teacher can't even fathom, helps us. We do run our households at age 12. How different our lives are from that of the other children in our class!

Sitting there in class, I think about my life now and how different it is from when my mom was married to Gene. I have experienced three different economic and social lifestyles so far in my short life: the first when my mother and Shawn were married; the second when she was married to Gene; and the third, this one, when she is raising us "herself." I am hoping this will help me in the future by giving me a broader perspective about life on Earth. It should help me relate to others better. I feel grateful for all the experiences, but certainly have my preferences. I wish with all my heart we were still in Gene's family, where I could have all the things I want and need physically and emotionally. I hope helping my mom struggle through school is worth all the work I have to do for her to accomplish that goal. I look forward to a better life in my future.

OUR NEW HOME

Later in the same year, my grandmother buys us a home in southeast Portland. It's a large, pleasant house in a nice neighborhood. I change schools to Creston Elementary. During this time, I fall in love with reading. My favorite books are biographies of famous characters in history. There is a large library in this school. During recesses and lunch, the librarian lets me read to my heart's content. I consume books, learning about many subjects. I love having this library to go to. Even though it is not as nice as the Hall of Records, it is a place of knowledge, and I am quite at home and happy in this similar environment. The librarian introduces me to Shakespeare, and I am enthralled with his stories. Every day, I look forward to my library visits. On weekends, I don't have that opportunity, so I take the bus downtown to the Portland public library. The entire day passes before I know it when I enter this incredible repository of books. I am in heaven in the library, so I visit often.

MY PET BODY

Adjusting to the new school is rough. Fortunately, I have a teacher I really like and that helps a lot. Making friends takes time, though, and is laden with problems. Although I don't really think about him anymore, Kuthumi's guidance earlier in my life saves me from many pitfalls of growing up. For instance, later in the year, some of my friends begin smoking. They try to convince me to join them, saying how cool it is and how good it makes them feel. I remember what Kuthumi taught me about my body being like a pet that I am responsible to care for, that I should listen to my body and take care of it because I am its guardian. This way of thinking about my body is very effective and helps me make good decisions about its care. As I consider what my friends say, I think that if my body were a pet dog, for instance, I would be crazy to even think of making it smoke a cigarette. My friends are persistent, but I am firm in my understanding that smoking is not in my highest interest.

Later, when the same friends become addicted, then they complain about how much smoking is costing them. They say they wish they had never started because they can't quit now and need more and more cigarettes. Then they try to get me to join them in what they are doing now, drugs and alcohol. I remind them how they wish they could stop smoking, but thought it was a good idea a few years earlier. I ask them if perhaps they will be wishing they had not done the drugs and alcohol in a few more years. I decide I will not get involved. I know I shouldn't give my pet body these substances.

My friends tell me I need to do these things to feel good and have fun. My reply to this is that I feel better than they do and have more fun without the substances. I am quite a bit happier than most of them anyway. They have to agree that I am a very happy person. Explaining to them that I don't need drugs to feel positive and it doesn't cost me anything (money or health) doesn't change their minds about it, though.

Sure enough, a few years later, these same people tell me how lucky I am not to smoke, drink, or take drugs. I just say, "Luck had nothing to do with it. I used my head to think it out, and it didn't seem to be a good idea." I can thank Kuthumi for that.

126

MEDITATION VS. DRUGS

While thinking this situation over, I find myself wondering if people did the exercises my teacher gave me to find states of ecstasy instead of doing drugs, etc., would they find it more effective. The meditative states he showed me provide mind-altering experiences and insight into life's challenges as well. This seems much better in all ways than drugs, smoking, or alcohol, and it has only positive side effects. Meditation is definitely life changing in many positive ways. I didn't think those substances could produce anything better.

I often sit quietly and wish with all my heart that others could learn the things my teacher taught me so they could experience the same peace and happiness he helped me find. I wonder if perhaps that training could help prevent these negative conditions and be a more effective way of alleviating their suffering. It seems to me, as I observe my friends, that they use drugs in an attempt to deal with problems in their life. It only makes more problems instead. This is a path of false hope, since it seems to provide few solutions for my friends. Meditative training works much better for finding solutions and has no negative side effects.

COLLEGE

At 16, I am very unhappy at high school, even though I am a good student. So much of high school is about social interactions that I care very little for. Attending Franklin High School in Portland Oregon is a trial for me. It is a typical high school, and I do very well there, at least academically. Socially though, I am restless. I can't seem to find a group of friends that I can really identify with, so I try all the cliques, one after the other. Since I am a school photographer, I attend almost every school event. This broadens my exposure, but I still feel very unfulfilled. It seems like I am seeking something, but don't know what.

Finally, it all comes to a head for me when I become ill with the flu. As I sit in bed, I turn to books and begin to read everything available in the house. The only new books are my mother's college books, so I start reading them. When my mother comes home, I don't even notice, as I am immersed in *Beowulf*.

"Tonya, I can't find my English literature book, have you seen it anywhere?" Mom says, as she enters the room. Seeing the book in my hands, she looks puzzled. "Oh, you have it. What on Earth are you doing reading that?" she asks, feeling a little frustrated about my taking her book, but curious as to why I want to read it.

"It's so interesting," I reply. "Your books and your school are so much more interesting than mine. I wish I could go to your school. High school is so boring, and everyone's into things that just seem like a waste of time to me. I'm so unhappy there that I don't ever want to go back," I state emphatically.

"Well I know how much you love to go to PSU and attend classes with me during your breaks from school, but you're too young to attend there. I'm sorry you're not happy with your school. I need to take that book you're reading because I have to study for my class, but I'll see if there are any other programs available for you in the area," She promises.

"OK, that would be great. I love it at your school because people there really want to learn. They don't at my school. They care more about who is dating who and what the latest gossip is about. I'm sick of it. I think that's really why I'm sick. I don't want to go back there. Please help me find a new school," I plead.

"I'll check it out," she repeats as she leaves the room.

"Thanks, mom," I reply gratefully.

The next day, she returns with good news for me. "Well, I found an opportunity for you, but it will be a big change, and you'll have to take the bus clear across town every day."

I reply, "Mom, I've been taking the bus downtown by myself for years, so that's no big deal."

"They have a high school completion program at PCC Sylvania campus. I checked and there are no age restrictions or rules that would prevent you from attending."

"That would be wonderful!" I exclaim excitedly. "You have to let me go to PCC. I know I'll be happy there. When can I start?" I insist as I jump up and down with glee.

"OK, as long as you keep your grades up, you can do it," she answers a bit hesitantly.

She registers me for the PCC program that same day. On the following day, I go to the high school to pick up my things, and visit the office to tell them what I am doing. When I explain the plan to my counselor, all she says is, "You can't do that." My reply is, "Yes I can, and I am. Goodbye." This is the very same counselor who wanted me to take home economics and quit my biology assistant position because she believes girls shouldn't be in such classes. I am so happy to be free from her grasp and the stifling, restrictive environment of the high school.

Later, I register for classes at the college and begin a new life that I absolutely love. It is the best decision I ever made for my education. After a successful year at PCC, I transfer to PSU, and finally I am where I always wanted to be, at my mother's school. It's like a second home to me. I move into the dorms there and have my own place for the first time. Here, in college, people think and discuss various topics of knowledge at length, and I am in "heaven" again. Although I put the memories of the real heaven world out of my thoughts years ago, little do I know that I will have an awakening soon that will bring those memories back into my life in a big way.

"Your pain is the breaking of the shell that encloses your understanding. Even as the stone of the fruit must break, that its heart may stand in the sun, so must you know pain." - Kahlil Gibran, *The Prophet*

CHAPTER SEVEN - PAIN AND THE AWAKENING MEMORY

SEEKING HIGHER KNOWLEDGE

The great love I have for learning and science leads me to continue my studies in life as I go on through college. I find I love psychology, but decide it is too easy for me, because I seem to know it already and get A's without trying very much.

Therefore, I decide to major in something that makes me really have to work my brain. I major in biology and plan to continue my education by attending Oregon State University in Marine Science for graduate school. Working with whales intrigues me the most. My life, however, is about to take a major turn; "fate" is stepping in on my behalf.

ILLNESS

During college, I marry Rick, a classical pianist and a fellow student at PSU. When I am eighteen, we have one child, a darling little girl named Reva. Shortly after I give birth to her, I feel something is wrong with me physically. When I go to the doctor, he says there is nothing wrong, although he hardly examines me. He does the blood pressure, ears, eyes, and throat routine. I return home and, a few days later, have to be practically carried into the emergency room with a 106° fever.

The doctors do not examine me much the second time either; they just tell me I have the flu, give me some codeine cough syrup, and send me home. On the way home, I have a reaction to the codeine that makes me hallucinate, so I return to the hospital again. They give me a shot to stop the reaction to the medication, and, for the third time, send me home.

I am very sick. For three weeks, I can hardly get out of bed. When I return to the hospital for my six-week postpartum check-up and tell my obstetrician what happened, she becomes livid and yells at me. "You're so stupid," she says in a very irritated tone of voice. "You needed help; you should have insisted they help you and that you be examined by an obstetrician the first time you came into the ER. You could have died."

I don't know what to say in response to her verbal assault, so I leave there thinking, "I am 18 years old, not to mention extremely ill, and this lady is telling me I should run the hospital. She is definitely off base." She gives me a prescription for antibiotics, and I return home. I don't ever go back to her again, and I begin to wonder about the proficiency of the medical system.

To make matters worse, I begin to have a series of kidney infections that never seem to end. For about two years, I go back and forth from the doctor's office in a scenario that repeats over and over.

First I feel that something is wrong in my kidneys; it doesn't hurt, but it feels like something is in them. I go to the doctor and he says, "Go home, nothing shows on the tests. There is nothing wrong with you." I protest, insisting that something is wrong because I can feel it and this is how it feels each time it starts.

The doctor repeats his same verbal denial. I tell him to look at my records, that I have been through this over and over, and I can tell when it is starting. He just says, "Well, it doesn't show on the tests, I can't help you," and sends me home.

Within two or three days, I return to the hospital emergency room, where I need help walking because I am in too much pain to walk on my own. Then the infection shows on their tests and the doctor gives me medicine, always antibiotics and always for 10 days. It's never enough to kill it off completely.

About the 12th day, I return to the doctor and explain that I can feel something still in my kidneys. He says it doesn't show on the test and we repeat the same process over again.

132

Since I am a science major in college, I begin to wonder if the doctor needs to go back and study a bit about scientific proof coming from repeatability. Then he begins telling me when it doesn't show on the tests in the first few days that it's all in my head. "If it's in my head," I think, "then why does it show up on his tests a couple of days later? Is it just 'in my head' for the two days prior to when it shows up on his tests?" I start wondering if he had to go through this a few times, would he think it's in his head.

Kidney pain is one of the most painful experiences anyone can go through. Since I have had it so many times, I must know by now, and I think it is worse than childbirth.

Kahlil Gibran, in his landmark book, *The Prophet*, wrote, "Pain is the breaking of the shell that encloses your understanding." Well, I can tell you one thing, it opens my mind to the fact that these doctors do not have a clue how to help me. I decide that if anything is going to change, it is going to happen by my efforts, and not theirs.

After praying for guidance, one day we are discussing the situation, and my husband teasingly says, "Well, why don't you go down to the health food store you're always going to and look for something that will help?"

I take him up on that idea and find a book there about a natural treatment for kidney problems. The book tells the story of a man who cured himself of Bright's disease. The book is called *Rational Fasting*, by Arnold Errett. His ideas are a bit radical, but I think, "It's certainly worth a try. What do I have to lose?"[*]

---

[*] If you would like to take steps to help yourself and take charge of your own health, read a book called *Own Your Own Body*, by Dr. Stan Maelstrom, and then read others as the spirit guides you. It is so empowering to know how to help yourself instead of having to rely on doctors and drugs. I have personally met Dr. Maelstrom. He is a true healer and a man with a great heart full of compassion for all mankind.

Later that afternoon, when my husband comes home, he finds me taking boxes of food from our cupboards to the dumpster. When he inquires as to what I am doing, I say, "I'm following your advice." He just shrugs it off and goes to listen to his music. I continue until I clear out all the junk food. Teresa visits later in the day and is surprised by how bare my cupboards are, but she encourages me on my quest to find healing.

Guess what? It works. I get over my kidney problems very rapidly, and learn, after a bit of trial and error, that dairy products and orange juice were the culprits. As long as I stay off the dairy and citrus products, I have no problems with my kidneys and do not have any more kidney infections. I have several close calls, though, when I eat things with dairy or citrus in them. I learn I can nip these infections in the bud by taking unsweetened cranberry juice and garlic from... you guessed it... the health food store.

SEARCHING FOR HEALTH

During all of this illness, my grades and marriage don't fare well. I end up divorcing my husband, quitting my bagel sandwich cart business, and, shortly thereafter, leaving school. Being ill is changing my life. Too much is happening at once.

At that time, I return to my mother's home for a period of rest and reflection. I become quite fascinated with the whole understanding of health. Although I am only nineteen, I begin to realize that the medical profession offers me little in the way of preventive health; it seems that it's up to me to find out for myself. I read about methods to assist me toward a healthy lifestyle. I begin to understand that without this basic health, I can really do very little with my life.

I have always eaten very well by American cultural standards, what is considered exemplary by most. In my studies, I discover that my love of ice cream, yogurt, and cheese, which I was consuming almost daily, was my worst problem because I am very lactose intolerant. Studying health books becomes my passion. I read everything I can get my hands on and learn much. It is fascinating to read about all those, who, like me, have become disenchanted with the medical profession and find help for their problems through alternative means of diet and medicine and a holistic understanding of their bodies.

Although it seems as if my life were beginning to fall apart, in reality, it is finally coming together. I do not realize it then, of course. I really enjoy my studies about health, and begin fasting on a regular basis.

During this time, as I am working on my health so diligently, I become associated with a health institute, The Green House, that educates the public about living a healthy lifestyle. After going through their program and being helped so much, I become a staff member and eventually end up running the place as their director.

I learn to teach classes on natural health, and meet a lot of people through this institute. Raw-food diet and wheat-grass therapy are at the heart of this method of healing. Folks come from all over the United States and the world to this center to study these methods. It is an offshoot of Hippocrates Health Institute in Boston and similar to Optimal Health in San Diego, based on the teachings of Dr. Ann Wigmore.

During these years, I learn a lot about how to keep my body healthy and prevent disease. The positive changes I begin lead me to many revelations about health and, following closely behind that, spirituality.

HEALTH TO SPIRITUALITY

While I am in the library reading health books, I begin reading spiritual books also, especially ones about the lives of saints.

Since biographies of great characters in history are a great love of mine, saints are even more fascinating to me. Some saints even had similar experiences to ones I had when I was a child. I believe I have discovered a gold mine. Each book I read helps me to feel more validated as a person. I am not alone. Finally I have found people who were like me and knew something about the heaven world and the guides or teachers. Their lives went beyond normal everyday living and they sought more of a spiritual experience from life. The more I read, the more I want to read. I am rapidly consuming books again.

After pouring through the entire collection of books on the topic of saints, available to me in Portland's public library, I begin looking for more. First I speak to the librarian; she is unable to offer me any more books.

HE'S REAL

While contemplating where I can find more books on saints, I remember Saint Ignatius Catholic Church, not far from our home on Southeast 51st Street in Portland. As a child, I often walked past their facility. It contains a school and monastery. Since I have attended catechism classes and occasionally gone to church there, I know several of the priests. I go there to see if I can borrow some books from anyone. The priest tells me that they cannot lend out books from their library, but anyone can come and read as much as they desire.

He leads me to a beautiful library full of books on saints. It is a very plush place with large comfortable chairs upholstered in velvet. It invokes feelings of familiarity, since it is similar to my heaven world library, but I am not conscious of this. I just know I feel good there and I like it. The colors of maroon, red, gold, and black dominate the interior decor. I have found another book heaven. Taking the most comfortable chair I can find and picking up the first book, I begin reading. Time

136

ceases to exist for me as I pour through the lives of people, who, like me, experienced spiritual things they didn't ask for and didn't necessarily understand either.

The number of books I read escapes my memory, but I finally come to one book that gives a shock to my soul, never to be forgotten. I find an old book of saints with pictures in black and white. Bound in leather, it has the rich feel of being an ancient treasure.

I snuggle up in my chair and begin to thumb through its pages reverently. There are pictures of several saints, so I decide to look at the pictures first. I reach about a quarter of the way through the book when I stop short, and, if I had been allowed to make any noise in that library, I would have gasped. Instead, I just hold my breath and stare in disbelief at the picture on the page in front of me. There it is, in black and white, a perfect picture of my childhood teacher, KUTHUMI. The name under the picture says St. Francis of Assisi. I am stunned, flabbergasted. It is Kuthumi. He is real.

I am happy, confused, curious, and excited. I sit there for several minutes; then I just feel like I will explode if I don't tell someone and shout it out to the world that I have found my teacher. Home is about ten blocks away, and I literally run all the way home. When I reach the house, I am out of breath, but I don't stop to catch it; I must tell my sister. She is sitting on her bed, also reading a book. When she sees my face, she knows instantly something is up. "I found him," I blurt out.

"Who," she asks, "who did you find?"

"That guy who used to appear and teach me about everything. You know, my teacher," I answer excitedly.

"What guy? Tell me about it. Show me his picture; I want to see too," she demands impatiently.

"You have to go there to see it," I say. "They won't let me check it out." She isn't feeling well as usual, so she doesn't go see it right away. But I am happy just to share this with my sister, who is still my very best friend.

We sit together for a while and talk about our childhood memories about "them," her auras, and my teacher. It feels good to reconnect with our past. After what happened when my mom found out, both of us rarely spoke about these subjects for about seven years. We discover we've both kept secrets. This time, we tell each other everything, the whole truth. I give her all the details of my experiences with Kuthumi and she tells me even more about the things she sees in people's energy fields. She can see their actions over many lifetimes, their soul history. It feels good to confide in her and speak the truth. Now, both of us want to find out more about our childhood experiences.

The book I find his picture in has a brief history of his life. Unfortunately, it has nothing that explains the relationship I had with him as a child. There is not much more information in the library at St. Ignatius. Their books have the same basic information about St. Francis over and over, but nothing that helps me find what I am looking for. I want to know why he contacted me, what those places were that I visited with him as a child, and who were all the other beings I met in that world. I have to find out and understand it all. Now that I know he is real, there is only one thing on my mind: to find him again and understand the things I experienced with him as a child. My search begins. I have to find him and I won't give up until I do.

This is obviously not the end of the story. It will be continued in the upcoming sequel:

Heaven and Earth
Book Two: Together Again

Glossary of Terms

Angels: Your guides: deceased family members, friends, teachers and certain beings who serve as helper beings as their chosen job in heaven. (See also Guides/Guardian Angels.)

Cities of Light: The cities of the heaven world of which there are many. They are often seen by people during near-death experiences. Also called etheric retreats, they are places souls go to at night, while their bodies sleep, for spiritual instruction.

Council: These are the beings who are in charge of overseeing those of us embodying on the planet. They have been called the board, the overseers, God, and the karmic board as well as other names. They are just souls who are further along on the path than us who are serving in that office to assist us on our path. You may be serving on a board for souls younger than you already.

Death Angels: Those who come to escort us home to heaven after death of our physical body. They are often relatives, and people quite often think they feel angels in the room when people out of body come to attend to their loved ones at the moment of death.

Devashan: The incredibly beautiful place you create for yourself when you get home to heaven. A place to rest and reflect on the life just completed. It can be whatever you want. However, there are no negative spaces in heaven; those would be created in the astral plane just above earth. Some souls do go to a negative place they make to punish themselves until they feel worthy to return home.

Earth: A denser state of being where we have physical bodies. A large school with many lessons for self-development.

140

General Soul Group: A group of about a thousand souls you are born with when you are born as a soul.

Guides/ Guardian Angels: Those beings who are assigned to assist a person in their lifetime. They watch over us, protect us and assist us in accomplishing our goals and gaining the most growth from our lifetime on earth. They are not to do it for us but to assist us in doing things for ourselves. They often provide us with inspiration and help us stay on our path in life. A loved one can serve as your guide. You can have several of these helper beings working with you over time and/or at the same time.

Healing Temple: A place where souls who have been through a severe trauma or anything that causes them to be extremely damaged go for healing in heaven.

Heaven: A higher vibrational rate than Earth. Where we go when our physical denser body dies, is sleeping, or is deeply meditating. A percentage of our soul remains there all the time even when we are in embodiment.

Life Review: This is a review of your life done with your guides and council members after each embodiment and whenever the council thinks it would be of benefit for you. It can be a review of just the one lifetime or several, or your soul development in general. It is to assist in your understanding of what you have accomplished so far and what you need to focus on learning in your upcoming embodiment and work in heaven in between, and who you will be working with. Since souls have different momentums on certain aspects they are often paired with someone who has attainment in something they don't. Hence the idea that opposites attract takes on a deeper meaning when you are assigned to them for your growth in an area.

The council members are very nonjudgmental and, often, you are the only one who feels bad about anything you experienced on Earth because you would like to have done better. The council and guides are very understanding and compassionate beings who are only trying to help you to do what is in your highest good. You grade yourself on how you did and then plan with these helpers what you should do in your next lifetime to develop yourself further. They do not work out the details but do make suggestions. You go and work out the details with your groups and they give final approval of your plan and may suggest changes. It is still your free will and nothing is forced. If you want to go to the higher levels where you have more interesting things to do and more freedom to do things you would like in your own way with more power and greater influence, then you have to pass the tests necessary to get to the next level from where you are. As my kids put it in the video games they play, you have to level up if you want more options to play the game with.

Light Body/Death Body: The fully lit body worn by a person after they leave their physical body and the death of their physical Earth body. It can sometimes take a couple of days for the light body to reach its full intensity after the body dies.

Portal: The space between Earth and heaven. Some describe it as a tunnel, some as darkness. It is the road home. It is also a vibrational frequency change that occurs during the transition from one world to another. Basically all is in the same "place" just on different frequencies.

Masters: Those beings who have mastered life on Earth because they have passed all the tests here and can now assist others to do the same.

Near-Death Experience: When the body dies temporarily, the soul exits and the person remembers the experience of what happened to them. Some go to Cities of Light, others do not. They often see things or know things that they could not have when they were in their bodies.

Overshine: Same as overshadow but with a brighter connotation.

Soul Body/Spirit Body: The body worn when we are out of our physical body and still in current embodiment on Earth.

Soul Groups: There are several of these I am aware of but there may be more.

1. **General Soul Group**: Is the group of about 1,000 souls you were born with as a soul. You progress along with this group forever. The larger general soul groups focus on a similar vibratory frequency that relates to a certain color and occupation. For example, I am in green-yellow soul group. Green represents healing, music, wealth, and visualization as a tool of positive creation. Yellow represents the accumulation and correct use of knowledge and the manifestation of joy. The lessons my teacher gave me were usually private ones. Those usually occurred on a daily basis. There were other lessons with my General soul group that I occasionally attended on various subjects. These lessons were not as personalized to me as the lessons with my teacher.

2. **Family Groups:** These are the souls in your general group that you work with the most lifetime after lifetime. They are easily recognized because when you meet them on Earth you feel like you have known them forever. Indeed, you have. You come back to Earth with them over and over, changing roles and developing different aspects of self. They usually have less than 100 souls.

3. **Mission Groups:** These are the groups of souls within your larger soul group who are working toward collective goals on Earth, goals like starting a hospital, running or creating a new organization, etc. They work together to help humanity in general, and each other individually toward the group and individual goals. They often have about 6-100 souls.

Teachers: Those beings who are assigned to work with souls to assist them in gaining knowledge in areas that they have competence in.

Thought/Feeling Transfer: The way most communication happens in heaven and between beings in heaven and beings on earth. The entire concept, thought, feeling, visual image and knowledge of what is being communicated is transferred to the recipient(s). There is no way to lie, but information can be withheld if a being would not understand it at their level.

About the Author

Tonya Gamman is an author, instructor, and stress reduction trainer. She is the owner of the Academy Of European Reflexology and Healing Arts in Issaquah, Washington, where she teaches classes on and assists people in healing using Meditation, Stress Reduction, Reflexology, Wellness Kinesiology, Reiki, and Intuition development. She also teaches classes around the country on the human aura.

She is the author of *The Flower's Secret*, a children's picture book about the cycles of life, reincarnation, and the importance of each soul's life. It is loved by adults as well, especially those who have lost someone dear to them.

She is married to Dr. Paul Gamman and they have seven wonderful children, Reva, Maria, Jeremiah, Joshua, Clare, Michael and Alexander.

Tonya is a counselor, reflexologist and regressionist as well as a reiki master. Her current passions are writing, helping people find healing, and the development of an alternative drug treatment program.

Her hobbies are reading, hiking, writing, dancing, traveling, and kayaking.

By Tonya Gamman
Illustrated by Rachella Devine

Once in a while an outstanding book is written that has great illustrations with a timeless message that transcends all age groups, all cultures. Tonya Gamman has written what some say will become a classic in its own right. It is the story of the life cycle of a rose. Yet it is more. It is about her mother's life-long dedication to generosity and helping those in need. The story is about how the journey of sharing leads to happiness and a sense of freedom.

This book also touches on the bigger picture of the Cycles of Life. The rose represents Tonya's mother as she goes through her own Life Cycles. One reviewer stated it so nicely when he wrote, "pure and simple beauty, a loving experience for children and adults." It is a delightful testament of a daughter's love for her mother.

It is the type of book that you want to get extra copies of to share with family and friends. It is especially valuable as a book given in memory of someone who has gone home to heaven and to help children understand death, life cycles, and reincarnation.

#101 New Swan Books, Paperback 33 pages 11 x 8, illustrated $ 7.95.

To order, email NewSwanBooks@Gmail.com